Stop, Change, Grow

Stop, Change, Grow

How To Drive Your Small Business to the Next Level

Michael Carter and Karl Shaikh

BEP

BUSINESS EXPERT PRESS

Leader in applied, concise business books

Stop, Change, Grow: How To Drive Your Small Business to the Next Level

Cover design credit: Charlene Kronstedt

Interior design by Exeter Premedia Services Private Ltd., Chennai, India

First published in 2020 by
Business Expert Press, LLC
222 East 46th Street, New York, NY 10017
www.businessexpertpress.com

ISBN-13: 978-1-95253-820-9 (paperback)
ISBN-13: 978-1-95253-821-6 (e-book)

Business Expert Press Entrepreneurship and Small Business Management Collection

Collection ISSN: 1946-5653 (print)
Collection ISSN: 1946-5661 (electronic)

First edition: 2020

10 9 8 7 6 5 4 3 2 1

Printed in the United States of America.

Abstract

Is your business stuck for growth or are you simply out of ideas?

This book is the inspiration you're looking for. In three major sections it shows you how to: STOP doing many of the things that were once right but are no longer appropriate, freeing up resources, allowing you to CHANGE what you are doing for better results today and then to GROW the business for a future that will excite you.

The authors came together in 2003 when they co-founded Virtual Directors Limited – a London based consultancy aimed at supporting small and medium sized businesses. They brought together 33 consultants from mixed disciplines, with talent ranging from rocket science, engineering and construction through to retail, corporate finance, HR and economics. Having also both worked on five continents, the authors have a wealth of experiences to relate in this book.

As you turn the pages, you will find real life examples together with easily implemented ideas and suggestions to provide an immediate impact on your thinking and your business.

Keywords

business; growth; controls; management; delegation; profit; improvement; start-up; stagnation; ideas

Contents

CHAPTER 1

Why This Book?

You've bought the book, you wanted answers for your business. Whilst numbers do vary considerably by industry and country, your turnover is possibly in the $1/2 million to $10 million range and the business is somewhere with 5 to 30 names on the payroll.

Your business has historically grown by leaps and bounds, but of late it is seemingly running fast, just to keep still. We see a kind of glass ceiling, where the other side is visible but tantalizingly unreachable. We call these Plateau Businesses. It's like driving a car with a punctured tire; you want to go faster, but unless you stop and change the tire, your speed and distance will be limited. Likewise, if you're on a road with lots of potholes, you need to stop and fill the potholes or consider driving along a totally different road.

Even if you see yourself running a lifestyle business, happy to remain under the glass ceiling, the Stop and Change sections of this book will make your life easier, freeing up more time and mind space for a better lifestyle. For you, there is the opportunity to skip the Grow section, although we suspect you might change your mind once you've seen the opportunities therein to use the freed-up resources to create a better business, and thereby a different lifestyle.

This book gives you answers. Maybe not the answers you thought you wanted, maybe only partial answers, and maybe answers you are not yet ready to admit as valid. This book is purposefully written in a conversational style, jam-packed with seemingly simple yet powerful questions and examples of applying this thinking in many real business situations. It's these questions, examples, and parables that are designed to prompt reflection, to help provide you a fresh perspective, and to help you wonder *what if I tried...?* It's up to you and your own curiosity to wonder *what if...?*

For Plateau Businesses, we've found that asking the right questions with a sprinkling of curiosity can do wonders to unleash your success. You already know it's not about "pushing harder." Some lines of questioning will feel irrelevant for your business—because we're not there in person to cut those out for you—whilst others will resonate and trigger you to take steps to move your business to the next level. For these steps that come to your mind, we've provided a handy Action This Today notepad at the end of the book for you to keep track of actions you want to take.

Oh, and by the way, congratulations, as 95 percent of all companies started have either folded before reaching the stage you are already at or still trying to catch you up.

Finally for here – if we have anything wrong or misquoted – please tell us and we'll correct it for the next edition.

CHAPTER 2

How You Got Here

Happily driving along one day, your car dips into a pothole. The subsequent clanking tells you there's a problem and you limp into the nearest tire center. Mechanics put the car on a hoist and you retire to the cold, drafty, poor excuse for a reception area. Fortified by a ghastly machine-made cup of something, you start reading a magazine article on the problems of disposing of used tires. They can't be burned and they shouldn't become landfill. Only so many are needed to be protection around motor race circuits or to be chained together to create artificial reefs in the sea. Minced up, they make a safe landing for children's play areas, but it doesn't use that many to do all play areas length and breadth of the country. Sure, some are remolded into new tires, but you can only do the remolding a few times before the whole tire is past reuse. So there are lots of unloved used tires accumulating in vast stacks around the planet.

Then, your Eureka moment arrives. You decide minced tires with a suitable binder/setting agent would be an excellent pothole filler, flexible yet strong, and not subject to deterioration in the cold. The only problem you have at the research stage is finding someone who will supply the small quantity of minced tire you want for your experimentation—multiple truckloads no problem, a couple of sacksful—umm problematic. A nearby, pot-holed, quiet piece of road provides a good proving ground for the Rube Goldberg output from your garden shed. You eventually find the right recipe and want to start selling.

Everyone thinks it's a great idea, but nobody wants to take it on, unproven. Finally, you persuade your local town council to let you mend their holes for free as a reference for others and, hey presto, snowball effect, after the next winter you have a fleet of trucks with your name on and a bigger gang of workers, earning you substantial sums nationwide.

A big construction company comes sniffing around. Their acquisitions director says they'd like to make you a wealthy man and take the business off your hands, if only, of course, post purchase, you'll stay on and run it for them. You think you can do better on your own.

But then revenues start to fall. You have filled in the largest potholes and they're not recurring, so work is dropping. You decide to hire a guru who, after much procrastination and no little expense, says "license the technology internationally," and there followed a sudden fillip in income, as royalties—mainly from Scandinavia—come rolling in. The next guru you hire says "diversify," so you take your best workers and set them on trialing whether the same product would provide good insulation if formed as house bricks.

You attend a routine management meeting. To your surprise, your local manager reports that without the best workers, the rest of the labor gangs are threatening strike action. The international manager advises that an obscure Japanese company is going to sue you for breach of their patent on a similar product. Your production manager tells you that when a road is to be resurfaced and the old surface heated to remove it, your filler burns and gives off toxic gasses. As a result, Health & Safety are threatening a criminal prosecution.

Should You Stop, Change, or Grow?

It doesn't matter if you started your own business, acquired it, inherited it, or somehow it landed in your lap. It doesn't matter if your business invented a better use for tire chips, or is a catering business, recruitment business, or fitness gym. Maybe you're in retail or wholesale. Or the business installs any variety of equipment into other business or residential premises. Perhaps it is some form of real estate or construction activity. There again, is it some form of professional, consultancy or service business? Or you develop online games, develop apps, have an online matching engine of some sort, or you provide training or education (online or offline). Whatever your business, you'll find many gems in this book either in the form of direct recommendations or posed as questions to trigger your curiosity to generate your own solutions—which we trust will be better.

The book is ordered *Stop, Change, Grow. Stop* is those little adjustments you might make at a red stop light or at a pit stop—like turning the wipers off. These adjustments should free up resources, time, mind-space, and make the experience of driving that much better. *Change* is where you might make minor like for like changes. Like changing that punctured tire. We think of these as resource neutral. *Grow* is like change of direction along a road you may very well have never travelled before, but with some confidence it will get you there. Or more like moving from a sports car as a happy bachelor to the family SUV to match your new responsibilities in life, knowing the two-seater will never again be part of you. The car swap may start with reluctance and apprehension ahead of delight with joy as you settle into the differences that come with the new car.

CHAPTER 3

Making this Book Work for You

This book is designed to be of practical assistance, rather than as a posy bit of management speak from a couple of university dons who've never left the campus in their lives.

We believe this book is full of useful questions, examples, tips, and hints, but even generically it cannot by, any definition, be comprehensive. If you have differing thoughts, try them. If you learn of other approaches elsewhere, try them too. Business is not logical because if the world was logical your business would already exist as someone else's. Likewise, business is not linear, that is, a business doesn't necessarily go the route intended or indeed in any predetermined direction.

Within this book, we have tried to create a stream. Small beginnings, bigger things later. But you have to determine if the stream is a rushing torrent or a meandering watercourse. Along the way, please pay scant regard to the section headings—a nugget in your stream might lurk behind a heading that would otherwise distract you. Likewise, however useful an index might be, it could easily be the authors have filing what you actually want behind a different word.

We also want to make it clear that we authors are not sexist—so where there is reference to *him* in the text, please equally interpret it as *her*. Whilst statistically most entrepreneurs are men, we want to encourage women into expanding their businesses too and don't want to put them off with our own brevity. Remember: "When God invented man, she was only joking."

Be warned, we do talk a lot about making widgets. But most of what we try to put across applies equally if you are a service business designing, coding, repairing, or trading widgets as much as it does to the manufacture of them. We use widgets to provide consistency in the writing, but can apply to any industry or service. Wherever possible, we use real industry and service examples including food, education, home services, retail, telecoms, agriculture, and so on.

If you are not used to widgets as a concept, think of them as a universal case. Like the use of Acme—meaning best—in cartoons, widgets can be something a farmer grows, a manufacturer makes, assembler assembles, a restaurant serves, a driver delivers, and a beautician pretties. It can be something programmed, written, recorded, produced, or broadcast. It works for a toll highway operator and a dress shop owner. Even allowing for the fact that we might not have listed your business or service so far, please believe, before we move on, that widgets apply to you.

Finally, for here, though we will come back to it, is the notion that you probably need, and think you are owed, a decent vacation. What can you do today to help that happen? If your business needs you so much that you can't take a vacation, you need this book even more than we expected!

Please enjoy, take action, and—oh, yes—a big thanks for buying the book.

CHAPTER 4

Start Now

In this book we challenge you a lot and do our best to trigger your curiosity and make you think *what if I tried...?* And then we encourage you to follow on with action. No doubt you will have thought about some of these things before, maybe in isolation. Our aim here is to nudge you into reviewing each of these areas with a fresh pair of eyes, to first free up some resources and free up some positive energy, before embarking on growth projects that will no doubt consume energy. Your commitment to a fresh perspective followed by real immediate action is critical.

So here are two questions:
Q1: Can you identify what your greatest asset is?
Q2: What is the biggest challenge your business is experiencing (whether associated with the asset or an unrelated aspect)?

Could you answer both questions in a couple of sentences?

By asset we mean things that are a source of advantage for your business—any of your premises, your staff, your patent, your unique recipe, your customers, your reputation, your unique way of doing things, your exclusive way of attracting and retaining the best talent, your pivotal location, your special relationships with other businesses in the value chain, and so on. Only you know what's special or unique in your business that is a source of advantage. Could it be something that your competitors don't have? Or may not have to the same extent or do as well as you do? Maybe it's you?

The point is, once you truthfully identify your one most valuable greatest asset, we can then work to make the most of this asset, protecting it and leveraging it further to act as a launch pad to add further value to your business. Meanwhile what are you doing to make the most of this asset? What are you doing to grow or build this asset? What are you doing to protect this asset? What are you doing to focus your own energy on this asset? Or are everyday distractions that seem to crop up demanding your time and energy instead?

It could of course be that the asset you immediately focus in on is the one that got you where you are today, but as time has moved on, its relevance has slipped. Perhaps it is time for a new #1?

As for the biggest challenge your business is facing, let's not guess right now, but either you know it, or if not as you work through this book, we will find your biggest challenge together. If you do have a challenge that comes to mind…try to describe both aspects of it: the change you desire *and* what might hold you back from achieving that change. For example, you could know improving the service you offer is do-able, but you can't afford to increase the level of service at the prices you offer. Something has to give!

If you can write those two sentences, relating to greatest assets and greatest challenge, please do so immediately. Then stop reading this book and go and deal with the identified problem right now.

Alternatively, you may prefer to make a note of them in the *Action This Today* notepad at the back of this book…and return to the rest of this book. If you know how to tackle these today, but you don't actually action these today, and put it off for another day/week/month, it is only ever going to fool one person—you. And you know the expression: "A fool and his money are soon parted."

If you are still with us, then you are in the majority who either don't know what is their greatest asset or their biggest challenge, or know them, but don't know how to make the most of the former or how to overcome the latter. And even when you think you have identified them, it will almost certainly require a fresh pair of eyes to begin to understand how to get best utilization of an asset or how to solve the challenge. This curiosity-inducing book is designed to help you tackle these and other questions to help you bust through the glass ceiling. For example, maybe you are famous for prompt local delivery. That makes your trucks and drivers the asset, but have you contemplated letting them deliver for other non-competing businesses in your neighborhood? Then they're earning when otherwise idle.

We think you get the idea.

CHAPTER 5

Stop—Before You Start

Initially we are looking at the status quo. We're looking to see if there are any obvious problems. We want to help you identify the limiting factors that have restricted your growth and brought you to this plateau. We're then looking to help you identify anything that you can do to free up resources and create positive energy and, more importantly than that, undertake any obvious fixes to what you are already doing so that you can retool for the next growth spurt.

Take a deep breath and hold it. Before releasing, ask yourself honestly: "Is it my people that are holding the business back?" As soon as you have an answer, release your breath and continue to breathe normally.

If you don't have an answer, you should by now have stopped needing to ever breathe again, and whatever your problem was, it is now someone else's—after they've arranged your funeral.

Hooray! You are still alive. If you have answered: yes, it's my people, then read on. We have a number of mindful thoughts that will help you with yours. But if it's not people, it is going to be the product, the customers, or the money. By all means, skip over the next section on people, unless there's a chance you're wrong, or that possibly the issue is some combination of factors which might surprisingly include the people dimension. Ask yourself, are people ever *not* part of the problem?

CHAPTER 6

Stop—*What If...It's Your People?*

When you started, everyone was excited and work was fun. But now, people are such a nuisance. You get good people and they quit; you get seemingly great people who quote the rule book at you and spend more time on vacations, maternity or paternity leave, sick and unavoidable domestic emergencies than they ever do working for you. In fact, looking around your business today, does anyone actually give a damn about anything, apart from you?

When you started, there was a small gang of you, dedicated to the company's goals. You all did everything or whatever was most expeditious at the time, and on the subject of time, no one was counting the extreme hours being put in, far less totaling them up as a basis to claim—heaven forbid—overtime from the business.

The chances are, given it is you reading this, that as the business has grown, you have grown with it—a seeming necessity—whilst the others have not kept up, fallen by the wayside, or fallen off the company bandwagon altogether. This necessarily created a void, and it is in filling that void and other voids in a like vein that you've created the monstrous problem your people now represent.

So where do we start with the complexity of people?

Legacy People

Do you have people on your payroll, acquired historically, but now retained just in case (JIC) or simply through inertia? Are these the people who prove to be most inflexible when you want to attempt something new and different? Steve Jobs has been quoted as saying,

What an average person could accomplish and what the best person could accomplish was 50 or 100 to 1. . .A small team of A+ players can run circles around a giant team of B and C players. . . In business the only viable strategy is to recruit good people, develop them and retain as many of the stars as possible.

Do a little mental spot check. Think about each one of your employees in turn, both good and bad, and ask yourself two things: One, what do they really do for the business on a day to day basis—and we mean really do, not what their job description or title says; second, what effect would it have on the company if any one of them unfortunately found themselves under the wheels of a truck later today?

The latter is probably far more significant than the former. Are they the unique holder of keys (think computer passwords as well as physical lock turners), knowledge experts for specialist processes, or are they your only link to an important third party? It is clearly time (long overdue) you got all of this documented or duplicated as appropriate, as your business is at risk if you don't. You mustn't have any indispensable people—oh yes, and by the way, that includes you.

Wow! That was quick—perhaps the single most important point in this book (so far), breezed over in a paragraph. Please halt just for a second to wake up to the criticality of having key people and whether their failure (including you) would mark the death of the business?

We suggest you go to the back of this book, and make a note to yourself of any action you wish to take on this.

But on the plus side, if you have documented and duplicated your "keys"—then by re-purposing the JIC staff—you might have the wherewithal to re-engineer the people side of the business and take the legacy element out by a switch to other more productive work. Or sorry to say, a redundancy program and showing the surplus individuals the joys of the other side of the revolving door of employment. Hopefully done in a nice manner, so as to help them in the next phase of their careers even if, right now, they don't seem to be helping yours.

Position Fillers

In larger organizations you are likely to have all manner of inward facing people. Accountants are usually the first of those through the door. As one of the authors happens to be one, we shouldn't rain on our parade—but we will. Typical accountants like to sit in their ivory tower, with an in-tray, a work area, and an out-tray. They'll say "good morning" to the bringer of the post and may grunt at another staff member in the kitchen whilst getting themselves coffee—if they haven't organized an underling for that—but aside from those interactions they prefer their own company to anyone else's. So a word to the wise, don't hire any such accountant. If your proposed accountant recruit isn't one that actively *wants* to go out with your sales force and win business (and secure the resultant cash in your bank thereafter) *and* volunteers this approach of his/her own volition at interview, don't hire him/her. If cash is king, then the accountants—and everyone else in your organization for that matter—is part of your rainmaking team—and the rainmaking process occurs all the way to cash in bank!

Likewise, the next most likely inward Herbert through the door is going to be HR. You will have got fed up with all the nonsense and quite frankly just the noise that comes from having staff and have decided to pass it all over to someone who can do these things properly for you. This will lead you to look for an HR person. Unfortunately, HR people—and yes, another derogatory gross generalization—are not good at taking this stuff away from you so much as becoming a conduit for it, back to you. Hire a freelancer, on a part-time basis or monthly retainer, instead. That way they are accessible to you and also to your staff when a problem arises, but they are not there to listen to, react to, and stoke the minutiae of tittle-tattle, on a daily basis. At interview, impress on them—and hold them to the fact after engagement—that you want early deliverables like up-to-date contracts of employment for everyone laying down the house rules clearly. You are not employing them to receive and report the next piece of gossip from the shop floor. Unless, of course, the information is material and important. But sorting the wheat from the chaff is what you hire them to do, not to make it your problem.

Up-to-date contract requires it to be not only current in terms of law, but also to recognize that this world now does most business via mobile phones and e-mail. Also that Facebook and friends are lurking out there and for all these you should have company policies, as much as the rules we are all familiar with in old contracts about making or otherwise of personal telephone calls during work time. Only then can they be allowed to organize personnel records and listen to the odd complaint, or start sifting through resumes for vacancies you might have.

To be fair to the wider HR community, the HR folk we have referred to in the above two paragraphs are transactionally focused HR people—as opposed to the other HR tribe who specialize in change management. We certainly like good, high-caliber change agents. They can be a huge ally and are to be welcomed with open arms, if you are too busy as we suspect you are.

So if you can outsource HR—which is what hiring a freelancer is—and you outsource your office cleaning, then for every role that isn't customer facing, isn't involved in production, or isn't critical to your asset identified earlier, always consider the outsource option. But never lose sight of the fact that *customer service is* customer facing—they represent your customers—so resist giving the duty of providing support for them to anyone else. It doesn't matter if all the customers want to do is complain—you need to know and listen, if you are going to ever do something about it. And of course if you don't, we wouldn't want to bet on your business's future.

Doing versus Managing

Finally, in position fillers, look at the top of each tree. Does your sales director have a sales quota of his/her own or do you allow him/her to sit in their office and simply manage the team? The authors found themselves advising a company with such a position filled by the company's hitherto best salesman and sales were dropping. After asking good questions it became clear that the sales director was making a complete hash of managing his subordinates, damaging their own quota achievement in the process. The solution was to demote the director, restore his sales quota, and have the CEO take over the people managing role. It worked, and everyone was happy, with the demoted director quickly out-earning his former self with commissions.

On the topic of sales quotas, CEOs should stop needing to have their own sales quota once sales people are hired. Because by default the accumulated sales quotas for all the sales people will add up to the company target whilst the CEO's focus should be on making the sales people as effective as possible.

Beyond sales, ask the same question for pretty much all of your people who have people reporting to them—are they productive themselves or merely staff captains? And is this what the business expects and needs? Sure, managing takes a little time, sure recruiting and inducting new starters deserves space in the schedule, but there's a good chance they have been promoted to the role because they were good at what they did and the question is: Is this particular talented individual being wasted in his current role? As a supplemental question, in a world of e-mail and direct responses, do these managers have PAs or other administrative support—whose main job now is simply fetching coffee?

Let's not lose sight of the moaners and complainers. They too are a dead anchor for your business and either need an attitude lobotomy or shown the route to the exit.

All this might be getting you ready to be thinking of a revolution—but we'll leave that for the Change section.

DIY?

When you started your business, you probably did many more activities than you were skilled to do. Do-It-Yourself (DIY) is normal when you are starting/running an infant or juvenile business. So when you have ideas for doing a new project, whether it's a little bit of additional marketing, or that extra piece of social marketing, for example, the chances are you probably taught yourself how to do it and tried your best to pursue that by yourself, in between all the hundreds of other projects you manage. And to be fair, that is the right strategy. Always take on a new project and do it yourself, for a while to really understand the role and how it fits into your organization, and then when you have sufficient insights you will know better how to hire the right person to make the most of that role.

In order to release some of your energy to achieve *real plateau buster growth* you will need to outsource these DIY activities to a specialist, even if the specialist himself or herself is a newcomer to this field. Why out-source to a newcomer, who probably can't do it as well as you, when you are trying to save money? 'Cause you need to release your energy for the bigger ticket growth ideas that will need your high abilities/creativity. You will also have more relatively low value-added work—which needs some-body other than you!

There is one other important people area we need to cover.

It Could Be You

Do you regularly feel that everyone is out of step with you? Do the others not recognize the priorities, they have a tendency to drop the ball at inop-portune moments and come knocking off time of an evening, whatever the urgency of whatever is partly complete in front of them, they then feel can wait until tomorrow?

If you find yourself nodding to some of this, don't you also find that the only action you can take is to sit on top of them as basically they can't be trusted and that consequently you are fundamentally doing their work rather than any of your own?

So let's be honest, could it be you? As an example, a software company we've worked with employs a core staff of about 10. By the fourth birthday of the business it was on to employee number 38. Not so much a staff turnover problem, more an open revolving door at the front of the build-ing. This company has a robust interview process on the way in—proven by the fact that two would-be applicants had even tried to charge for the day's attendance to do the company's interview assessment tests. So it's not that. Surely it can't be the wages paid, as a new recruit wouldn't join if the pay didn't reflect his then view of his market worth. It cannot be the hours because those are the standard 40 per week with very few extra hours over-time worked. So what's the problem?

It's the boss. The staff can't fire him, so instead they leave. Now if the boss-man ever sat down long enough to compute how many frogs he'd kissed to find a princess—or in this case how many interviewees to find a new staff member, multiplied by 38, he'd perhaps realize the truth and then take time to consider whether he ought to hire someone to do the people managing rather than him.

No, we don't mean setting up an HR department; just have someone, perhaps promoted from the current team to be the 21st century equivalent of a foreman—and then channel everything through him or her. Maybe expand the role and let this person do the legwork on hiring as well and perhaps he or she could also be allowed to talk directly to some of the suppliers, customers, and stakeholders. Then are we shooting for someone more akin to a Chief Operating Officer with documented delegated responsibilities? Alternatively again, perhaps the boss should get out of the business from an operational perspective, completely. Hand the reins to a CEO or whatever business leaders are titled in your industry. And sit back as simply a shareholder.

Don't agree? Let's consider a few more symptoms that might point to you being the problem.

Do you wake up early in the morning yearning to get over those personal and household chores so that you can get to work—the source of all your pleasure? Or do you lie there in bed, not sleeping though exhausted, with your brain rattling through a never-ending loop of business issues that are all clamoring for your attention? Do you then take your insomnia to work, exist under a dark cloud, and unfortunately bark at staff and customers alike?

Then there's vacation. Do you even remember what they are? Of course you do—they are those things that get you riled when members of your staff take them. But how about you yourself and taking a proper vacation? Have you taken one in forever? What is your favorite excuse for not taking one? And given you haven't stopped work for any period in years, doesn't this mean your batteries are flat and actually, you are not at the top of your game?

The authors know of a UK company owner who took a two-week break to a Thailand beach. During that time, he became part-owner of a bar there. By e-mail and telephone, he then made a number of adjustments to the UK business similar to some of those in this book and has basically not gone back to his UK business at all. He still works to support his UK business mainly by telephone with customers and, with time differences, starts early and is finished by lunch. He certainly feels the benefit of his prolonged vacation.

And then there is the famous work/life balance. Are you ducking out of family and social engagements because of work? Whilst sometimes this is a convenience, sometimes it is an assault on your conscience—or even a stream of abuse from the smitten one(s). Do these latter reactions affect how you behave toward your staff?

Pause: Did you make notes of things in the Action This Today section in the back of this book? If not, please take this opportunity to review the prior pages to identify again any thoughts and ideas you want to follow up on.

CHAPTER 7

Stop—*What If…*It's the Product?

Wait. Don't skip this section because you think you are a service, not a product. Does a restaurant, for instance, have product issues? Maybe you specialize in steak—surely that's your product and if you offer too many or too few choices that may be your "product" issue. Alongside steak, do you offer too many or too few alternatives? Are the vegetarian choices obvious? Does the menu need a complete overhaul? Would a new restaurant name, or a new theme, or simply redecoration help?

Having some of these thoughts in your head will help you as you go through these pages—and don't think because you run a landscape business and not a restaurant they don't apply either. Or to you, if you are a firm of architects, accountants, doctors, scientists…

Product (or Service) Reality

When you came up with your original product, it wasn't actually *original* but it was certainly innovative. When widgets were only ever available in gray, you produced them in Day-Gloop yellow; where they'd only been right-hand threaded you made them ambidextrous and where they were only ever sold in boxes of 100, you launched the handy 10-pack.

The market liked the color change and although multithreading has advantage to a few, for most it was simply a *nice to have* feature. The 10-pack didn't just break bulk for those wanting smaller quantities; to your relative surprise it was taken up by many of the bigger users too, as it kept the product safe from wandering hands and the widgets chemically clean inside their hermetic seal.

At launch, you created an ocean of clear blue water between your business and the competition. Whilst perhaps the widgets didn't initially fly out in the volumes you had hoped for, we think it safe to say that after that piece you did on television, they were selling handsomely.

You were probably right to stick to the single color, as adding color variety was only going to increase your costs and cannibalize your Day-Gloop yellow sales. Costs needed control because although sales growth was good, costs have been climbing steeply as well and for a while there was a chance of you overtrading. That is because you were frequently having to pay your bills before several of your important, larger, customers paid you.

And you are still making the same product today. Volumes are not as high as at the peak, even after adding in those specials you now do for a few important customers.

Why? What might have gone wrong?

It could be simply in this age of enormous upheaval in the geopolitical landscape, many of your customers have now opted for dual-sourcing in case you (or the other supplier) for whatever reason—from Icelandic volcanoes exploding to unrest in a country of raw material source—fail to deliver on time.

But that's unlikely.

It could be that actually Day-Gloop yellow is no longer a fashionable color—but we doubt that too. Maybe your widgets are being underpriced by some cheap, nasty imports. No, we've not seen many imports of any quantity show up on these shores.

So stop and look really hard.

Just as you do specials for important customers, so do your competitors. They're not in the competitors' literature—any more than they are in yours or even referenced on respective websites—but they do them. Similarly, there is off-slalom pricing, extended payment terms, long-term contracts, and similar devious tricks all designed to win, to win back or simply for your competitors to retain existing business, so that new customers for you are no longer *low hanging fruit*. Therefore, if you lose one through defection, change of business, or bankruptcy, replacing it with two others, as you used to do, is no longer easy-peasy.

Strange to say, that's only part of it. What has almost certainly happened is your competitors have innovated past you. Not simply copy-cat-style improvements like offering post-box red or grass-green widgets.

No, they've gone much further. The market leader now offers a completely threadless, self-sealing widget at the same price as their previous model. They guarantee their customers a 50 percent saving in assembly time and for only pennies more can provide a digital interface so that their widget can be monitored in real time by anyone with a Wi-Fi connection.

You won't have missed the publicity razzmatazz for these innovations but you have probably dismissed them as both gimmicky and something you cannot compete with directly, as you are still a few years away from paying off the financing, for the tooling, of your original widget?

So we imagine you've tried to guess the future and work out what next year's widget will look like so you can shoot for that and gain competitive advantage. But can you?

If you look back on your own launch, you hit the market with a Spanish Armada style broadside. The market had been stuck in its repetitious rut since, we don't know, let's say the war? Maybe the Civil War? Your revolution awoke a number of slumbering dinosaurs who probably didn't realize the rest of the world, like you, regarded them to be in some sort of long-term terminal decline.

Your innovation should have destroyed the competition but instead led to some amazing invigoration. Hence where you are now. Fighting the established giants, who seem to have come back against you stronger than you could ever have imagined, and with better widgets than you. How?

Again look closely at what you did. You brought step-change to widgets. After implementing this strategy, you had planned post step-change—and doubtless by now have introduced—a number of additional changes along the way as the market swung toward your widgets. But what were these additional changes? More step-changes? No, we're sorry to tell you, they were cosmetic—more akin to rearranging the deck chairs on the Titanic than reviewing the true capabilities of watertight doors.

Meanwhile your competitors were faced with the *innovate or die* conundrum. Those that picked up the challenge went to the suppliers of widget-making technology and specified their next generation of widget tool, to not only be up and over your step-change but also be capable of making further step-changes in the future. So there you are. We've told you. You brought the first significant change and your competitors have gone for future change-proof constructions.

That means the time period, or in the parlance, first-mover advantage, is much reduced and rather than playing catch-up, you are in a market where leap-frog is the game. Worse, alone out of all your contemporary competitors, you can actually make fewest future step-changes.

And it is not all fiction. One of the author's clients did indeed steal an early first-mover advantage by the simple expedient of buying in bulk (in his case 200s) from the manufacturer and repacking in customer-friendly dozens. Of course it didn't take long for the manufacturer to see the market opportunity for themselves…

Stop Leading the Incremental Innovation

Look carefully. Are you in a market where incremental innovation costs you disproportional time, money, and your personal energy, yet this increment is probably not recoverable from your customers? Doesn't that make it a lose–lose for you? What's more, in such a market it is probably easy for a competitor to replicate your ideas and quickly return to level peg you.

Why not reverse the roles and wait for their incremental innovation first? Then you can promptly introduce *only if* your customers desire it. So rather than start the competitive surge by throwing the first stone on anything incremental, think of the alternative gain by not throwing it at all. And potentially keeping the savings for the next disruption (covered in the Grow section of the book).

What do you have to lose? Ask yourself what happens if you slacken the pace of your updating of the standard widget?

Well, first, you have your special customers, the ones whose widgets require sophisticated changes to the core design. The ones who appeared as bright opportunities initially, but by the time you had built the first widgets that conformed to their final specification, you really wished you hadn't started. But you have them, you are over all the initial pain, you have made or paid for all the special tooling, and your workforce can now bash them out as easily as your mainstream widget.

These guys are loyal—they have to be—because their production cannot easily change unless you were to hand over the tooling. And, of course, you're not going to do that. They also don't want to see massive innovation in the product because what you supply now works for them and all the other components that go in alongside your widgets into their final product. So look at them as a cash cow—that is a product that remains unchanged into the future, continuing to supply an existing customer base providing valuable margin to you without constant attention. And you won't have to load its pricing to pay for future product step-change.

Second, and with this slowdown it is the bit you are scared of, a few of your more exciting, cutting-edge, customers might move away. You like these guys, they like you. You're all chummy and you believe the product gets better because of your frequent interactions with them resulting in new ideas. But actually, in total they don't buy very much and, however strong their opinions, they are not opinion formers for an industry, they are simply legends in their own lunch boxes.

The third impact of you slowing your pace is far more remarkable. Rather than being left behind by a bunch that barely sentences ago we wanted to write off as dinosaurs, you will find they slow the pace down too. In a race with no end, it is the pace-setter that determines the speed and the running pack just tuck in behind. After you slow down the incremental innovation, and if your competitors tuck in behind you, then you take the pace-setter role, but at a slow and steady manageable pace. However, if they relish themselves instead in the pace-setter role, you tuck in gently behind them, taking advantage of their wasted energy in incremental innovations that are easily replicable by you. Either way, you reduce your energies allocated to maintaining an incremental innovation pace and apply that energy to larger things discussed in the Grow section.

The good news from slowing down is that inertia will keep most of your customers loyal to you for far longer than you ever imagined, even if you don't put as much as a toe in a forward direction. On that basis most of these guys can be looked on as cash cows too.

Look at the Bigger Picture

Then, climb aboard your business helicopter and go for a 10,000-foot view of your activities. No, we don't mean a real one; this is brainwork not joyriding. From a detached perspective, ask yourself the final product–related question here: Is the market for widgets finished? Because if the answer is yes, you have to decide between them being a cash cow until people stop buying them or if you are fast on your feet, a great time to sell up. Holding on for the nostalgia market might be a one-way ticket to oblivion.

If the answer is no, then give a thought to disruptive innovation. True innovation has to be disruptive. That's what a step-change represents. A new way of doing business like using mobile phones we all have now instead of holding pocketfuls of change for use in phone booths, as we once had to do. Or a price reduction. Not *by* the odd 10 percent, but instead *down to* 10 percent of the previous price. Disruptive is not a little bit of styling or a modest tinkering with the price. It's not evolution; it's revolution. Stopping incremental innovation frees up funds, energy, focus, and all-round mind-space for you. Replacing it with disruptive innovation will consume most of these, and we will cover that as a topic in the change section.

Pause: Did you make notes of things in the Action This Today section in the back of this book? If not, please take this opportunity to review the prior pages to identify again any thoughts and ideas you want to follow up on.

CHAPTER 8

Stop—*What If*...It's the Customers?

While growing up, one of us worked in an old-fashioned ironmongers' store. It was a lot easier to keep the shelves stocked without customers; it was easier to keep the floors clean without customers and, at the end of the day, adding up the money in the tills was foreshortened without customers.

QED, customers are the root of all evil.

No, they really are. Look at most small business failures. They typically fail because they run out of money. Why? Because their customers haven't paid them. Start-ups fail through lack of customers, but bigger companies fail because of them. There is an old adage that "any customer is a good customer"—but that's baloney! It might have been true at the ironmongers that another bod through the door could be sold another handful of nails, weighed out and put into a brown paper bag (we did tell you it was old fashioned), and that additional sale would generate both margin and more importantly cash flow ahead of paying wages on Fridays, but it doesn't work today unless all your business is for cash.

And, thinking about it, even then, the customers who got the biggest discounts—I mean the only ones who got any discounts—were the trade customers—and guess what? They had credit accounts! Now we're betting that even if you claim to be a cash business, you will still have some people who don't pay you at the time of delivery with rectangular sheets of numerically inscribed pieces of rectangular paper issued by a government (i.e., money, if you are not one for "cryptic" clues). Or perhaps in this technological era, proffer you a piece of plastic capable of being processed at an electron level, into a value transfer to your business bank account.

Customers Take Credit from You

Our guess is most of your customers/clients/patients, or whatever is the correct terminology in your business line, take time to pay as you have intentionally or otherwise granted them credit terms. More that, although you've had the odd bad debt, you haven't insured your debtors against default—probably because you are as cynical as we are about the insurance game. For those that don't know, you pay insurance premiums for years but when you do finally have grounds for a claim, the insurer wriggles and wriggles, trying to find ways to *not* pay you out. Therefore, to our minds, why bother in the first place—we think it sensible to keep insurance cover confined to covering those potential catastrophes which would destroy you financially if they occurred and those insurances you are obliged to have, by law. But this decision must be yours; you don't have to agree with us on this, or indeed anything.

Like us, you probably didn't go to a credit reference company when you first acquired the customer on the grounds that any data they have will be based on history rather than what's happening now. Likewise, any supplier references the customer might have given you at the time would have been from a couple of their tame suppliers who only ever said nice things about the customer.

Pardon? Surprised! Yes, we are, as you *did* use a credit reference agency in the beginning. But are you getting regular (or even annual) credit reference updates for the 20 percent of your customers who doubtless provide more than 80 percent of your revenues and, significantly, are 80 percent of your debtors?

> Helpfully, the dear old 80/20 rule is often extremely close to the mark with all things to do with customers. Try it. Do in fact 80 percent of your revenues stem from just 20 percent of the customers?

Look the other way too. Does 80 percent of your grief/cost/headache stem from 20 percent of your customers *and*, for the double jeopardy prize, how much of the first 20 percent generating your revenues overlap with a second 20 percent listing of those who give you the most hassle? It might surprise you to see how little overlap there is.

There are several corporations around the world though mainly in the United States and frequently in financial services, who historically would routinely sack the bottom performing 10 percent of their staff. So why don't you mutate this strategy and get rid of your 20 percent most troublesome customers and get 80 percent of your life back?

Doubling Your Margin?

That's not very scientific. Nor actually is revenue generated a good basis for decision making. The crux of the value of any customer to you is the margin you make from each—the difference between the selling price and the costs of providing whatever you do for the customer including a sensible apportionment of staff time and overhead—the time that wouldn't be used if that customer's activity dropped to zero.

Margin will factor in the discounts you give away, the freebies you throw in to support the customer (co-marketing, promotional, or whatever this extra spend coaxed from you by your customer is labeled by both sides in the transaction), and not forgetting after-sales service cost. It is only the margin derived from each customer that will pay your costs and hopefully help you make a profit. And even then, the margin can't pay for any of those things unless the money is in your bank account, so perhaps in calculating the margin (do it for say a year—a good time base) you should also deduct a sum equal to the average increase year-on-year of the amount they owe you at any one time. This latter item is the margin tied up in your debtors and therefore not available to the business.

Now, assuming you can do this, ask yourself proper searching questions about any customer on your list that comes out with negative margin. A searching question is of the form: Why should I continue with them? Rather than: What's the next entry in the bumper book of excuses that I can use to justify retaining them? If it was going to be the hairy old chestnut of: if I didn't have them, my competitor would, then we'd say let your competitors have these loss leaders.

Hopefully, there are no loss leaders. Now look from best to worst at the rest. How far down the list do you have to go to capture 80 percent of the total margin? Our guess will be 20 percent of the way down the list. So if one-fifth of the customers drive most of your margin, why were we further up the page looking to shed only 20 percent of our customers? Let's do simple math on losing 80 percent of your customers. Losing 80 percent of all the customers really would give you more space to go find some new ones—even if you're not ready for such a big step right off the bat.

With the extra time we have created (dropping 80 percent of customers), it could be possible now for you to go out and secure a few more customers with the profile, that is, volume, margin, and ability to pay, that you want. Even if you simply acquire a new 80 percent with your old customer profile, then 20 percent of 80 percent, that is, 16 percent of them, will be in the same league as your previous top 20 percent. Now if we do the math: 20 percent (old) plus 16 percent (new) is, dear friends, a virtual doubling of your business margin.

Mathematical mumbo jumbo you say? Yes, it would be if you tried to gain new clients before dropping the burdensome clients. By now you know the premise of this section of the book, right? *Stop* doing certain things to free up time, resources, mind-space to then grow, if you want to. Let's try this. First, fire these 20 percent of low-margin clients. During that process, you might instead be able to renegotiate, increasing your sales price substantially, thereby improving your margin and make you want to retain them. Then, use that spare capacity in your sales time and freed up mind space from those gone, for new customers and voila!

OK, perhaps you don't do the firing wholesale, if you feel timid. Fire them at a pace that fills you with joy and see your margins improve.

Apply the same rules each year and you'll find you're increasing the average value—to you—of each of your customers. Remember *no* customer has any automatic right to buy from you, so you don't have to be charitable, or in some cases, put up with some of the nonsense that you do.

Pause: Did you make notes of things in the Action This Today section in the back of this book? If not, please take this opportunity to review the prior pages to identify again any thoughts and ideas you want to follow up on.

CHAPTER 9

Stop—*What If…*It's the Money?

"I can't grow the business, I have no money to…" is a frequent cry. But before you're bumping up against the glass ceiling of: I have no money, you're most likely first hitting the glass ceiling of lack time/resources/energy. We know that doesn't seem to be the case, but what if it is? That's why the Stop section so far focused on those nonmoney issues. Once you have implemented the relevant recommendations in the Stop section covered so far, you will have freed up time/resources/energy to be ready for growth.

And then you are ready to rightly ask yourself, if there is anything I need to Stop, to stop leaving money on the table? And we've got you covered in that department too. First by considering recommendations about cash, and then on the next section considering recommendations about price—which is perhaps the most underestimated source of money by most business owners—but more on that later.

As we have already identified, it is the margin you make on the sales, translated into cash in your bank that gives you the tool—money—to do what you want/need to do. It's the absence of this money that risks you overtrading.

Overtrading is easy. All you have to do is spend all your money on inventory and then regardless of how much demand there is for your product, or whatever fancy prices you are charging your customers, until some of them actually *pay*, you have no money to buy any more inventory, or meet your wage bill, or pay for any other overhead. So, there's a risk you'll go bankrupt and leave a lot of potential money on the table for the liquidator to collect badly instead.

And talking of nonpaying, do you have customers who don't pay you until they want to order from you again, and are you then perverse enough to persevere with them and their little game? If so, new rules. The customer prepays future orders or they take no further product from you.

Factoring and Discounting

Let's just check you have already researched either one of the two related opportunities of factoring and discounting.

Invoice factoring is selling all your invoices to a finance company, which then advances you a largish percentage of their face value upon receipt of invoice, paying you the rest when the customer settles up with them.

Confidential invoice discounting is where you sell the finance company the invoices but the customer doesn't know—they still settle with you—and you settle with your discounter once you're paid. The discounter still gives you a large percentage of cash on day one, but you are better able to control the collection process. Obviously the confidential invoice discounting only works if the discounter approves of your systems and trusts you to return its advances.

With either method of funding above, unless you have negotiated non-recourse terms, if the customer ultimately doesn't pay, you get the invoice back and have to reimburse the advance you had earlier received against it. Non-recourse is great, but you've got to have one hell of a quality order book and a broad spread of customers for the factor/discounter to agree to work on that basis. Even if they do take them off your hands—with no comeback—you'll frequently be stymied by the seemingly unrealistic credit limits that finance companies place on each of your favored clients. It's no different to insurance really, because that's what non-recourse is.

If you're not using one of these, then why not? Having say 70 percent of your receivables in your bank account rather than *out there* must make sense if you're always short of money.

Stock-Turn

But let's not get fixated. Apart from covering your anticipated short-term requirements, it is almost certainly better that your cash is tied up in saleable inventory for customers that do actually pay you, than sitting in the bank. Then your cash is at least working for you—assuming your pricing allows for attractive net margins—rather than kicking around in the bank earning paltry interest—if any. Again, note the words *saleable* and *pay*. Unsalable inventory is another name for landfill; nonpaying customers are worse than a bad joke.

A lot of businesses require inventory to function, though obviously it is of considerably less significance if you are a services company or a software company. You'd be surprised though. If you are an architect, do you have a lifetime's supply of the wrong-sized drafting paper? As a restaurant owner, what's been in your store room since time began? Almost everyone acquires some inventory irrespective of the type of business, so don't rush to deny it. But either you do, in which case read on, or don't and you then skip this section, having paused to remember the meaning of the three-letter acronym (TLA): JIC. For those of you tempted to skip ahead, thinking you don't have inventory, do you have any "spare capacity" in any aspect of your business?

If you don't think you have inventory, as you read the next piece try to substitute the words "spare capacity" for inventory. Yes, spare capacity is very different from excessive inventory. It's not true substitute, but like excessive inventory, spare capacity is leaving money on the table in that some of your assets are underutilized. We feel that if you allow yourself to be creative, this substitution might still help you unearth a few interesting recommendations for yourself.

Inventory is stuff you hold in anticipation of a sale (or to build into a sale) that you are storing at considerable cost, but which could conceivably be better left with its manufacturer. Look at the auto industry. Forty years ago when there was a genuine industry, each company took pride in building pretty much every component themselves, in-house. However, the risk of strike action, the inability to match supply and demand, and so on, led to each of these manufacturers into building huge storage complexes to handle fluctuations and to ensure that the production line had weeks of supplies on hand. Nowadays, autos are assembled from components made by subcontractors and, in accordance with best just-in-time (JIT) principles, the subcontractors are sent orders electronically today, for tomorrow's assembly-line requirements. Inventory levels can now be measured in the auto business in hours' worth rather than in months or years.

So why have you got so much of it? Why shouldn't much of it still be cluttering the original manufacturer of the stuff, rather than you having to not only find space to store it? Worse, you are also having to finance it as well. Reaching for the well-worn, bumper book of excuses we can see JIC trying to win out against JIT. That's pathetic. If you went over to JIT, and JIC actually happened (and it rarely does), surely you'd still manage to get the required item(s) from its manufacturer/supplier in plenty of time to satisfy your customer. A good way to ensure this and make it the supplier's responsibility is for you to agree with them an SLA (service-level agreement) preferably negotiated when you first start trading with them, detailing *their* commitment to reacting to changes in *your* demand.

"It's not inventory stock-turn which is the problem," we hear you retort—though in truth it often is. Much more likely, however, is that you were hoodwinked by the original manufacturer or supplier into taking more than you need at any one time because of their seeming insistence—by word or financial inducement—to make you take minimum quantities of a line, make up minimum order sizes, or have you fall for one of their promotions that transfers their overstock problem on to you. A consequence of that is you almost certainly have a lot of money invested in saleable inventory but that it might be some years before much of it gets sold by you. Perhaps 80/20 applies here too: 80 percent of your sales come from only 20 percent of the inventory—which is regularly replaced—whilst the rest just stays around from one annual stock take to the next.

With a Little Help from Your Suppliers

One way to potentially deal with the excess, if you accept that your manufacturer/supplier—who always insists *you* take a minimum quantity of each item—actually has opened cartons (for instance) in their warehouse because they will supply odd pieces of inventory either to their own retail customers or as warranty replacements for faulty items, and so on, then there is a potential deal to be done. If you can identify what you hold in inventory but which in your hands doesn't sell from one year to the next, you then ask your manufacturer/supplier to take those items back. If they are current lines, they should—but always be ready for a sharp intake of breath from them.

Maybe this book should be titled: *A breath of fresh air* as you might be entitled to ask why each time we hit a big decision, breathing is involved? There is no obvious answer to that one—though most other *refreshing* solutions involve brands like Coca Cola—no, let's not go there. But just maybe it gives you the really positive thinking time you needed, in clearing the head. There is science to support the notion of deep breaths being helpful, as University Of Michigan's Health blog suggests:

> Diaphragmatic breathing calms the nervous system and releases tension in the body. ... By releasing endorphins, the body relaxes, and you feel more comfortable. Boosts energy and increases vitality. As you breathe deeply, you increase your energy levels and allow fresh oxygen and nutrients to be distributed to your cells.

So breathing really does help.

Back to our supplier, in originally shifting the items to you, they made a profit on it; then to give you a refund or a credit now will, in effect, mean them giving you back some of their previously banked profit. So expect their expelling of breath to occur in parallel with a jumble of words headed in your direction and where you'll find the two key discernible ones are bound to be: restocking charge. A restocking charge in effect gives them some margin on the returning items to replace the profit they're handing back to you, and when they resell the items again, they'll make a new profit too.

Now from a cash perspective, suffering a restocking charge is worthwhile because it turns products which are tying up your cash into spendable cash. But from a profit and loss perspective (and if pedantic, the absolute total amount of ultimate cash in your business too), this restocking charge by them is a loss for you. So here's what you do. You say "will you waive the restocking charge if I spend all of the credit amount on new inventory?" There's certainly a negotiation to be had here. Try it.

But do make sure that what you are buying next is that 20 percent of your inventory that moves quickly and so you will be able to turn it back into cash for yourself within the next sales cycle.

And next time their representative comes to see you with a great price, if you will take a large volume, say "yes" to the deal, but demand that you call it off (i.e., take delivery and pay) in bite-sized chunks over the ensuing weeks (or months) and so have it as you need it rather than all upfront.

Everything is negotiable until the other side says it isn't. The question then is whether to switch the same conversation to an alternative supplier. If the supplier in front of you wants your business, it should be on *your* terms.

Overheads over Your Head?

It is easily possible for a customer to have historically wrapped you around his little finger and persuaded you of the wisdom of doing him a "one-off" or "special." It hopefully led to great things, but we would suspect that your business would now be better off if you hadn't had your arm twisted, because it didn't finally lead to great things. Are we right?

Hindsight is a great way of beating yourself up, but to no advantage. Better to use the lessons derived from looking back, to look forward.

There is no doubt that, unless your business is high-end jewelry, commodity trading, or stockbroking, people are your biggest expense. That's why there's the section about people—and it's quite a long section—at the beginning. So we won't provide a repeated summary here except to ask, *Do you have people on your payroll, acquired historically, but now retained JIC?*

Similarly, do you have underutilized assets JIC? Are your premises now too large for what you want to do? Perhaps you sublet part or move somewhere smaller? Do you have too many premises? A branch office perhaps when you thought it important, retained now JIC? Or are you renting/leasing/owning a number of places in this locale, when one site would be a better way of doing things? *Are you hanging on to somewhere for purely legacy reasons, when a fresh pair of eyes would see it rather more hysterical than historical?*

As a restaurant, could you create space for a delicatessen in one corner? As an architect, might it make sense to sublet an unwanted office to a quantity surveyor? As a realtor, shouldn't the art on your walls be for sale, as your visitors will soon have blank walls to fill? For our widget maker, would some sensible pallet racking or a mezzanine floor installed in the warehouse shrink your total ground floor area needs and then allow you to revisit the sublet question?

The same sorts of questions apply to your fleet of cars and trucks. Are you holding on to any of these JIC? Should you do your own distribution at all? When did you last have a third party quote to take all of that chore away, particularly if you are taking part loads, long distances. Clearly someone else could consolidate into their loads built up from a variety of sources and at least reflect some of their savings back to you.

Now it is time to ask the questions of your plant and machinery. How much of that was acquired for business you no longer do and would its release put any cash back into the business and potentially free up some space for the future or to sublet? And look in those dark corners and the back of the yard. We're talking about the stuff you really aren't using and never will again, yet you never finally disposed of?

And then, do you remember all those fliers you have had from the *we check your utility bills* companies which you've binned over the years? And all their blood-sucking, leech-like properties are lost to you when, had you called them up, they'd have given water, power, telephone, and so on, the kind of review of these expenditures you've kept promising to do and never had. Given they should only work on a percentage of what they save, why not give them a whirl, now? *But as with everything, read the small print as paying a fee of one year's savings might be fair, but committing to an ongoing fee for ever might be a rip-off.*

Pause: Did you make notes of things in the Action This Today section in the back of this book? If not, please take this opportunity to review the prior pages to identify again any thoughts and ideas you want to follow up on.

CHAPTER 10

Stop—*What If…*It's the Price?

Do your customers only buy from you because of the price? If the answer to that is yes, then we suggest you stop trading now, fold the tent, and go and find something else to do with your time and energy for the rest of your life. Unless, of course, you are using price intentionally and for a limited period to gain market share. Should that limited time have expired by now? Sure, the price has to be in the ballpark—and some ballparks are extremely narrow, but we really hope your customers are buying because your product or service is better, your supply is more secure, faster, and delivered free, and your credit terms are better (careful with that one), because you have a great relationship and you actually listen to your customers or, as we identified before, your customer is dual sourcing in case you or the other guy can't supply for whatever reason.

Pricing Right

Pricing is in the *STOP* section of this book—as opposed to Change section—because we have found that most businesses in your position need to stop leaving money on the table and thus release some money into their business. When did you last raise your prices?

Let us ask again. When did you last raise your prices and make the increase stick across your entire customer base? And what's your industry doing? Iron ore companies have industry wide annual price fixing with their customers based on whatever is negotiated freshly each year rather than simply last year's price plus a percentage increase. For most other industries, it is unfortunately left to individual businesses who will otherwise get themselves into enormous legal trouble if they collude on this matter.

Some businesses can get help. Many professional services organizations publish annual surveys of fees charged—are yours above or below the survey average? Do you write fixed term and fixed price contracts with your customers—or do you add in a little clause allowing for an annual review in line with/larger than inflation and/or interest rates? Or for international trade, in line with/larger than exchange rate variations? And if you do include annual reviews, have you been implementing them?

Any pricing for any customer has to be a win–win. If the price is hurting you more than it's hurting the customer, then you need to sit around the table with the cards face up and negotiate a better deal. Or simply announce a price rise—particularly if, in the doubling your margin section, the calculations show you are hugely into negative territory. If you know your customers—please tell us you know your customers—you'll know how to implement a price rise with each in turn.

If you are a restaurant business, a change of menu might be a good time for a price review. Some other businesses might establish a practice of annual price changes which they might use as a sales tool—*buy now before the increase* and so forth. We have a local coffee shop which increases its prices annually just as a big local tennis tournament arrives, benefitting from higher volumes and higher margins during the competition and then leaving the new price in place for the next 51 weeks.

Unless you have some commissioned sales people, every penny of a price rise flows to your bottom line—provided always that you keep the customer and the customer keeps paying.

Our guess is that your pricing has been built up higgledy-piggledy over time, and a comprehensive review is long overdue. In fact we implore you to look at every aspect of pricing triggered by our comments in the few short paragraphs above. However, this might not yield the sparkling total you would like to see at the end of the rainbow, so maybe there are still other factors affecting cash.

Pause: Did you make notes of things in the Action This Today section in the back of this book? If not, please take this opportunity to review the prior pages to identify again any thoughts and ideas you want to follow up on.

CHAPTER 11

Stop—*What If...*You Do Something Different?

There is that wonderful classic tale of a couple of U.S. tourists who, whilst driving their hire car are lost in the back roads of Ireland, so they stop to ask a local farmer for directions. He tells them: "If you want to go to there, I wouldn't start from here." Likewise the same might apply to your business. It might not be the business you wanted. You might have inherited the family business but rather than work it, you would prefer to be a rocket scientist. It might be your business has become a lifestyle business and that you've had enough. Or that you set up a landscape gardening business to use some of your creativity and now all you seem to do is repetitive lawn-mowing contracts. Or you set up to create exotic ice creams or cakes and today over 90 percent of sales are still vanilla and chocolate.

Sell Out

We could hypostasize forever, but if you are a square peg in a round hole, you might prefer to stop rather than grow. But stop is rather extreme. If you've read this far, it is a fair bet that you have created something with a value and that with a little more effort you could realize that value for yourself as opposed to throwing the whole thing in the trash can. So instead, *what if...you* sell your business. In doing so:

We should stress that a little effort and patience from you can materially alter what you can achieve from the sale of your business.

Let's consider a few pointers to increase the selling price:

- The best sales price is usually achieved for a going concern, that is, trading and healthy with no major problems existing or on the horizon, and ideally with growing profits. So if you can encourage revenues, if you can resist unnecessary costs, then you'll improve the profits which add sales value. Normally one can expect to achieve an increase in sales price by a multiple of any profit improvement.

- The business will sell for more if you can personally be taken out of it without materially damaging its business levels. In that event, your drawings, wages, and other costs associated directly with you can add to the bottom line for the buyer. So try to ensure you are dispensable, not the operational focus.

- A buyer in a similar business might pay handsomely if he can bolt on your sales to his business, but dump all the costs. That might leave you with some clearing up tasks, but think of the money.

- A buyer will pay more for a business that looks clean and tidy. So maybe dump the junk in the warehouse or back-room. Maybe mend the faulty whatever. A new coat of paint? Replace chipped crockery. Dump the problem customer, put flowers in reception… It's your business and it's your list of tasks needed—you *do* know what we are talking about.

- Be positive around potential buyers and don't panic. It is unlikely they'll make you an offer immediately, but a favor-able first impression is vital, so that they want to come back and negotiate.

- Statistics indicate there is a strong possibility you will already know the identity of your buyer. Therefore, take a little me time and generate a list. Ensure you think outside the box and spread the word.

- Have you thought far enough outside the box to consider selling to your staff? If they can't afford to buy, why not rent it to them and have an income whilst pursuing something else with your life. And still be able to sell later.

Failing all else, and you can't sell the business, are the assets that make it up of value as individual items? A family member of one of the authors was the youngest member of a funeral business and, at 75 years, a little old. There was no business to sell on as everyone else had retired. But in the business was a 1929 Rolls Royce car, which when sold provided a nice pension.

Seeking to sell warts and all is a sure-fire way to get the fewest dollars from your sale.

If you are planning to sell up, do spend a little preparation time on the question you are bound to be asked by your buyer: "Well then, what are you going to do next?" No purchaser will want to know you are selling up only to start the same business again in competition.

If these suggestions are not enough, the Grow section includes making an acquisition. If you think of an acquisition as the opposite of a sale—which it is—you will find the acquisition pieces also useful in shaping your sale plans. That's because if you examine your business through the lens of an acquirer, you should be able to see—and deal with—any likely area of complexity which could drive down the price, without waiting for a buyer to do that in front of you.

Recycling Is Not Quitting

If you still want out, but really, really can't see how to extract even one cent from a potential acquirer for what you have in place already, there is another alternative other than closure.

Recycle. Stop your business doing what it is doing, right now. Tomorrow morning investigate each asset you have—people, equipment, premises, processes, customers, brand, deep relationships with others in the value chain, and so on—and allocate it a role in whatever you want to do next. Sure, there will be redundant parts but the pieces you are capable of reusing are surely less expensive than buying new (if equipment) or hiring and training (if people). You are also avoiding all the administrative hassle of incorporating the new business, registering it with authorities and utilities and all that nonsense involved with setting up new banking arrangements. It is also much less disruptive if you are retaining some or all of your previous customers.

We bet that *Jackdaw's Chicken Shack* reopening as *Jackdaw's Thai Kitchen* would retain a tidal wave of customer goodwill that would not be available if the name became *Thai Palace*, for instance. And that loyalty is going to save you many thousands in advertising.

Still Don't Know?

Within this Stop section, we've considered the people, the product, the customers, and the money. You must have found some affinity with some of those issues and the odd nugget in the portfolio of suggestions. You will have read that you can *Stop* doing what you are doing, at least long enough to catch breath. Whilst enjoying lungfuls of fresh air, you looked externally as the world has changed immeasurably since you last checked and then will have examined your team, your tools, and yourself. Have all these factors changed in your company too, anywhere nearly enough, to keep your business ahead of the world? You've already reviewed pages of initiatives to consider and implement. We see these opportunities as a chance to free up headspace and create more time, energy, and resources for the next stages.

But you want more. *Change* is what is required now. Several changes are overdue. Some are big ones requiring steely resolve as you won't be able to undo them later. Some might appear small but will give you scale advantage later. Changes we identify should be neutral in operation in terms of energy and resources required so that if in this part you find something that'll work for you, don't wait to finish the book, just get on with it.

Later to *Grow* will take investment in energy, money, and focus rather more than anything else to set the platform for growth. If you've got the right people, the right tools, good suppliers, and customers, you've got the mandate to shoot for the moon. Let's show you how—but first, Change...

Pause: Did you make notes of things in the Action This Today section in the back of this book? If not, please take this opportunity to review the prior pages to identify again any thoughts and ideas you want to follow up on.

CHAPTER 12

Change Starts Here

Unless you have been asleep, we have already outlined dozens of things for you to have looked at and, if appropriate, suggested some corrections you can make. If we are together on this, you should already have freed up resources which we will ask you to later invest in growth.

And if you haven't yet taken action on those, it's because change (and yes Stop is a type of change) always has obstacles holding you back—we'll call these Opposing Forces. If there were none of these Opposing Forces holding you back, you would have already made those changes way before you picked up this book. Yet, you've picked up this book because the changes you desire are illusive.

Opposing Forces

What's an Opposing Force you ask? It's a military term used for a unit tasked with representing an enemy, usually for training purposes in war game scenarios. Once you identify who the Opposing Forces are, what their objectives are, and where they are, you can then go about overcoming the Opposing Forces. If you skip the initial identification stage, overcoming the Opposing Force tends to become more difficult. You need to know what/who you're up against to stand a chance of overcoming it/them.

Likewise, when you have a desired change in mind, you need to first identify the Opposing Force, before you can overcome it. Let's take it for granted that any change you desire already has an Opposing Force. If an Opposing Force didn't exist, you will probably have already successfully achieved the desired change.

In military training scenarios, as your proficiency increases, you'll be exposed to increasing difficulty levels of Opposing Force. Likewise, in business we see three levels of difficulty of Opposing Forces.

- Puzzle: The change you desire is of a relatively simple *Cause and Effect* variety. You're working with a one-dimensional relationship. Once you understand the cause and effect relationship, the Opposing Force can be easily—though maybe with a little effort and more data—identified. The Opposing Force has a simple answer with clear criteria. So you know where to look for answers and what type of answers you are looking for. Checklists and textbooks are good for dealing with puzzle-type Opposing Forces.
  - An example of this might be to determine what the tactics are for getting the best return on investment (ROI) of your marketing spend in your specific type of business, assuming you have a predetermined marketing budget?
- Problem: The change you desire is of multidimensional variety. There are multiple possible answers that require judgment and choice and rarely can be answered with simply getting more data. It's complicated. Checklists and textbooks are *not* sufficient for dealing with *problem* type of Opposing Forces. Relevant experience to understand the potential second- and third-order implications of what you choose to do is what you need.
  - An example of this might be deciding whether you increase your marketing budget or allocate that increment to other projects that might/might not have a higher return on your investment and these other projects may or may not have a positive or negative effect on your marketing initiatives.
- Mystery: This is where the Opposing Force is invisible. You do *not* know who or what you are up against. You're in an emergent and unpredictable environment and have no clear answers to choose from. These options defy definition and clear criteria. They are complex and you cannot know the effect or the Opposing Forces until you have the cause so you're in a circular argument.
  - An example of this is finding your business on a plateau!

We think you're a dab hand at dealing with puzzles and can give most people a run for their money when it comes to dealing with problems. However, as you embark on busting through the plateau, the Opposing Forces you are dealing with are by definition invisible. You do not know who or what you are up against.

Yep, it took us the whole Opposing Forces section, or just over a page, to say that if you're a Plateau Business, then by definition you are up against Invisible Opposing Forces.

In military situations, if you don't know who or what you are up against, the priority becomes to send out a reconnoitering team to scout out the terrain to gather knowledge to figure out who and what you are up against and where they are located. Likewise Plateau Businesses need to prioritize experimentation or, if you prefer trial and error, to figure out what you are up against.

We can't offer you predetermined solutions. That is why the premise of this book has been to encourage you to think: *what if...?, how about...?,* and let's *try this....* We can offer many parables to facilitate alternative perspectives and enthuse your curiosity to overcome the Opposing Forces, whether visible or not, that are holding your business back.

We said earlier—truthfully and intentionally—that this book is *not* written by a couple of university dons. It means in part we have purposefully been light touch on a broad range of hopefully useful topics rather than narrowly focused on one. And we have no intention to quiz you on it later. Instead what we want is to inspire you to burst through your plateau. Our continued objective in this book is to select a few things that inspire you to curiously identify things that will allow you to experiment, and with a better insight of the Invisible Opposing Forces, make bigger bets and get maximum impact.

It is important you actually take action. If you read this book—or indeed a far more comprehensive book—without taking action, that would be a total waste of your time. We don't want to waste your time.

We've tried our best through the words on these pages to help you look at these changes from different perspectives—because we know that you already know deep down in your gut you need to make these changes. We have and will continue to pose questions of the *what if...?* variety to help you overcome the focus on the hurdles to changes. Let's now be more blatant! How much do you desire the fruits of the change, and how can you overcome the hurdles to change?

We'll now look at more big-bang opportunities before reviewing some other meaty chunks of change. Some of these will require very little effort on your part, some considerable planning, but we rather see these as, on balance, neutral in terms of the energies needed to implement them. Their rewards should be anything but neutral.

> What is important is once you have identified those changes you are going to make, start on them and don't leave them parked on some imaginary to-do list. Commit to these changes. If it is your business, you are the driver of change.

CHAPTER 13

Change: *How about…*the People Inside?

But we haven't yet finished with introspection. There is no point being radical in the world if you haven't first and continuously been radical back home. Are there any tasks or processes within your business that need a fresh perspective in making them better? And let's divert here for a second. Continuously radical is a commitment you make to yourself to constantly re-examine every facet of your business to see if there's a better way. Better doesn't need to mean leading edge—the best data capture device we ever created was for a group of florist shops, to collect all the delivery notes, supplier invoices, and suchlike needed by HQ and which were frequently going astray. It was a humble spike. Once spiked, none of these documents were ever lost, and when finally released, they provided a complete record. An additional bonus was the documents were also already filed chronologically, which, when dealing with queries, proved invaluable too.

What Do They Do?

We have assumed above that you do actually know what each person does. There is a theory that effective management/delegation best follows the rule of seven, meaning each person to have no more than seven direct reports. If you have seven and each of those have up to seven themselves, you have a maximum sized company if evenly spread across activities of $1 + 7 + (7 \times 7) = 57$ people, before necessarily creating another level. If you are fewer than 57 souls, it must be reasonable for us to assume you know what they all do. Because if you don't, then we suspect you already have legacy passengers or position fillers.

Of course the rule might simply be a piece of MBA speak we're working so hard to avoid, but it does ring true with many of the companies we know and work with. Up to that sort of number in your team, you should know what's going on in some detail.

Maybe Hire Slowly, Fire Fast?

The chances are, as you spend time deliberating over letting go of a person, who *may* not be up to your usual high standards, you will lose five plus of your better people. The reality is these better people will be frustrated working with this person that doesn't match their high standards either. And what's going through their minds is that they shouldn't waste their talents working for a business that tolerates a person like *that*. The best people want to work with other great people. Seeing your tolerance of subpar performance signals to them, they are in the wrong place. The best people are always the first to prioritize their careers and move on.

Callous and cruel perhaps, but if these JIC people are eating into your profits, contributing less in return, and tempting your best people to leave, then they're not part of the business; they're part of the problem. If you are actually into charitable giving, then we think you are entitled to pick a charity of your choice, rather than it being chosen for you by continuing with these people.

When we were employed in a national coffee business with sales offices and warehouses nationally, it acquired a rival national business working from a single center. Our fellow directors wanted to retain the acquired business premises and team JIC. The authors argued successfully against this and proposed that by passing out the acquired company's customers to the existing regional operations, it improved their efficiency, whilst for the customers, it offered better service through its own higher quality people. It made no sense to keep the acquired premises, nor its people JIC. JIC of what? It would be like hiring people en masse which would have lowered internal standards. It's better to hire slowly, being as sure as possible the new hires fit/exceed the standards set by your team.

Before you rush to fill that vacant spot, how can you truly figure out if the candidate truly can walk the walk on personal accountability:

- Commitment: the willingness to do whatever it takes to get the results desired.
- Resilience: the ability to stay the course in the face of obstacles and setbacks.
- Ownership: unwavering acceptance of consequences of one's actions (whether individual or collective), with zero blame or argument.
- Continuous learning: seeing both success and failure as fuel for growth.

What Do They Think Needs to Change?

A few braver, bolder owners/CEOs of businesses we know make it a habit, usually on a monthly basis, of taking a recently hired member of staff out to lunch. Not the same person. The idea here is to rotate this one-on-one right through the company, and it's not to be a direct report either because there should be ample one-on-ones with such people in the normal course of business engagement.

Now it is very nice if this is a new hire, because it is a great way to make them feel really welcome to the company—but no, leave that responsibility/honor/pleasure to his/her line manager. Though do make sure this does happen. No, instead you want to get them three to six months in—you'll know the timing better than us—when they know pretty much how your business ticks and their part in it, they still remain enthusiastic and haven't quite forgotten their previous career and the inspired parts of it. Of course if they are already moaners and have left their enthusiasm way behind—there's a different conversation to be had, and it's not over lunch!

And no, it is not simply good enough for you to make the observation that you were involved in the individual's recruitment, and that you have exchanged the odd greeting around the water-cooler. What you want is to let them tell you the good and the bad as *they* see it now, which means you must *shut up and listen*. Sure, you will often have to set a framework, prompting at different times to have them focus their commentary on their job, their line manager, anything they want to tell you as the bigger boss, and so on. They might have methods or ideas they remember from previous employment that could benefit the business or have become aware of wasteful processes within their current role. After all, we shouldn't have to constantly reinvent the wheel.

You should also allow them to eat the odd morsel before their lunch gets cold. In return, you'll be able to feed back to them, between mouthfuls of dessert, what a great job they're doing, noting minor course corrections and so on. You will doubtless know all the facts to support this piece, because we can be certain that all of this will have been told to you by their line manager, just before the lunch in question. We never cease to be surprised how often the manager—operationally between you and your guest—suddenly realizes you're lunching with someone in his or her team and feels the urge to brief you.

The purpose of the lunch is to have a clear understanding of what's really going on in your business from a people perspective and therefore be able to continuously make informed decisions on people matters. And, when you do gird your loins and go for a big-bang change, to know the right things you will have to do to keep the right people.

Strange, but nice strange, things happen when you do this sort of thing. We authors know of a CEO who lunched with one of his sales clerks and, directly from her resultant enthusiasm, she introduced from her own circle of contacts the three next hires for the company. And of another CEO who took the accounts assistant to lunch with the above intentions and later married her.

What Are They Saying?

As a rule, people rarely complain to you about the person standing between them and you in the company hierarchy unless that third person is rude, abusive, demanding sexual favors, or displaying other inappropriate behavior. If that third person is simply hopeless, or ineffective, or not listening and responding to comments from below, there's every chance you won't be told. Sure, that lowly worker will sound off to his contemporaries, his family, his drinking buddies, or whatever—maybe even looking for another job elsewhere, but he or she won't tell you, the only person who can actually change things.

So listen carefully to subtexts in any encounter you have with those outside of your direct reports.

One other way of barometer checking is the company meeting. Invite everyone, make it during working hours, and after updating, praising actions, and announcing business developments to the multitude, open the room up to discussion on ideas for improving the business. Obviously respond to what is being said, but try to also be aware of any sections of your business not contributing en masse as they might be suppressing comments or obeying line manager orders. Similarly, be alert to where suggestions from a section don't seem to get a ringing endorsement and support in the same meeting from the person who nominally heads that activity.

And please not just the one meeting. They should probably be a regular occurrence and you can bet in the first meeting, there'll be a lot of nervousness and reluctance that slowly dissolve as people begin to feel more comfortable with such sessions over time. And if that all seems too formal for your liking, have an "impromptu" meeting whenever there is a new hire to welcome on board or when you have just won a major contract or whatever. Don't make it a session in a local bar. It is not the right place to discuss company secrets quite apart from the fact some might not enjoy (or perhaps be old enough to enjoy) a bar atmosphere.

Pause: Did you make notes of things in the Action This Today section in the back of this book? If not, please take this opportunity to review the prior pages to identify again any thoughts and ideas you want to follow up on.

CHAPTER 14

Change: *How about...*the Product?

Product Changes

Be open to change. Just because you (or your industry) has always done it this way doesn't make it right, today. Or maybe is it done some other way elsewhere? In our steak restaurant we cook out back on electric. Meanwhile in Argentina they'd cook out front on charcoal. Who's right? More importantly, be curious. What if you stopped doing it the way you've always done it? Can you try it differently and be inundated with a following of new customers?

Or imagine for a moment you own a chain of delis. Your specialty is cheese and you have large refrigerated display cases full of cheeses for your staff to cut portions off for customers. You encourage your staff to discuss the various flavors to ensure the customers get exactly what will suit them best. Then, perhaps at lunchtimes, your stores get busy. People perceive it will take too long to be served, which is particularly annoying for them if they know what they want without having to listen to the spiel again. They leave, you lose that custom and possibly that customer forever. So why not have a few handwritten cards describing cheeses in displays of precut, weighed, and priced portions created when the stores are not busy? And perhaps maybe an offer of "paired" crackers to go with a particular cheese. Perhaps too, to indicate the right wine for a cheese, and stock that too—or provide a link to a wine supplier ... Whatever your product or service, we encourage you to relook at it with a fresh pair of eyes.

So Where Do You Go?

First ask yourself … should your widgets or related processes be and are they not:

- Simplified: Are many of the features nice to have rather than necessary, and would removing them to a more basic configuration gain customer approval?
- Deregulated: Can you make a version which doesn't have to comply with needless regulation especially where it is not used in that particular field?
- Exported: Helping yourself to some government-sponsored support for export might mean you can sell beyond these shores.
- Replaced by software: Maybe a stretch, maybe the inspiration you need.
- Utilized: Do you have spare capacity that could be utilized in other ways?

For widgets, perhaps becoming a subcontract manufacturer for a rival to get better use of your expensive plant. For a restaurant, sharing the seating area with an adjoining business. For a local newspaper, forming a buying group with other regional titles to buy newsprint better. We could go on. We trust your thinking will.

Be Disruptive, Again

We're imagining you arrived with a bang, not a whimper. Though of course you could have built slowly and gently and for you many of the thoughts below apply too.

Disruptive: You took the widget market by surprise, your entry wrong-footed the incumbent suppliers, you won immediate market share, and now you are—let's face it—an incumbent too. That's why in the Stop section we suggested you stopped incremental innovation, because all that is now is a race to standstill, and if you are leading that race you are spending money you haven't got, to force your rivals to spend money they'd rather not, just to match your pace. But if you don't innovate, will they innovate? The question therefore is: what next?

The answer is to Be Disruptive, Again.

Imagine for a second you are at a local charity bazaar. The entry price lets you place your name and telephone number on one square of a large Treasure Island map grid. The winner, to be announced much later, is based upon some predetermined square where the treasure, that is, the prize, is deemed to be buried. A similar treasure map exists for your widget business. The difference is that for you there is more than one elusive prize and therefore you have to determine where to concentrate your initial grid work. On Widget Island, you could try Organic Beach, Integration Peak, Geographic Cove, Doubling Bay, and Sellup Landing. Offshore is Hooksky Island and various reefs in Lottery Lagoon.

If you feel with widgets that you've already been there, done that, got the tee-shirt, you might instead want a completely new playing field and go offshore where you can be disruptive again. Hooksky Island of course is just one of the options open to you.

Let's just call this: Hookskys.

What do you mean you know nothing about Hookskys? They've been around almost as long as widgets and the production of them is as backward today as it was when you walked into the widgets arena all those years ago—and actually, it is a few years, isn't it? There are lots of synergistic considerations, too. Just pause for a moment: Your staff would use similar skills in radicalizing that product and market; many of your existing customers purchase Hookskys and you've got the space to make them.

Maybe some examples might help. Accountants have overlooked the arrival of QuickBooks and more latterly Xero amongst others. Accounting software programs have usurped a lot of practicing accounting firms' bread and butter to the point where almost every start-up rents the software rather than uses an accountant for its bookkeeping. Likewise for lawyers, the Internet has made a mockery of the once noble art of legal drafting. Specimen contracts for almost any situation are now available for $39.99 or less each online. We bought 2,500 different drafts for less than $300 the other day! Veterinarians can't have failed to see how much of their once lucrative accessory business has now gone to the mall-based or online, pet mega-super-stores. And we could continue, sector by sector. Please give this more than a moment's thought. Does this ring any bells with what you do?

There's much more to say, but are Hookskys the "x on the map" you were looking for?

Pause: Did you make notes of things in the Action This Today section in the back of this book? If not, please take this opportunity to review the prior pages to identify again any thoughts and ideas you want to follow up on.

CHAPTER 15

Change: *How about…the Customers?*

Organic Growth

A minority of you will say "No, Hookskys are not the answer to my question" as either you started from scratch or picked up an early-stage company and over many long years, through good times and not so good, have gently grown your business to what it is today. You aren't into this disruptive game—there's no Thomas Edison or Henry Ford in either yours' or your corporate's DNA. Instead your "x" is on Organic Beach.

There's nothing wrong with this approach—it's invariably how almost anyone in private health or professional practice as examples ply their trade and grow their business. With the amount of red tape out there and which is seemingly added to on a daily basis, we truly respect your achievement and persistence to date.

By our reckoning, a goodly portion of your growth potential has been syphoned off even before you got near to winning it. And we haven't yet considered limitations placed on you. What if your business itself is the limitation? Say you have 500 arable acres and you simply can't grow any more crops, so your turnover can't increase and you certainly don't want to hire any more staff. Or that you can't extend the delivery range of your fast food service because there are no more dwelling units within range of keeping the food still warm whilst being delivered. Or perhaps your franchise only covers a limited geographical territory? These are all poor excuses. Here are some examples of more fresh perspectives we've been encouraging in this book:

- If you're good at growing stuff, lease someone else's land to add on to your estate or consider growing higher value crops.
- If your produce is used in further processes by others, why not start doing some of that extra processing too and make your product more valuable?
- If you are delivering fast food further away, how about selling it cold and raw and gain the advantages of, first, a lower price to make and, second, let your buyer do the *freshly cooked* bit in his own home.
- And if you have a franchise (ugh—we don't like franchises) and it's working well, acquire another concession area.
- If not a franchisee, offer other people a franchise of your business.

On that last point, we are often asked about franchises. There are some great ones. Who wouldn't want a McDonald's franchise—knowing that before you open the door there is an established customer base well aware of your offering. But why would McDonald's or indeed any franchisor offer a third party—you—the opportunity to make money that they could earn for themselves? The answer for some of the smaller ones is they don't have the money to expand. For the ones you've never heard of, it is because they want you to work long hours for below market wages to help build their brand. For McDonald's and its ilk, clever people will have established how they, through both the franchise price and control of ingredients, marketing, and pricing, probably end up being equally profitable whether running the place themselves or letting you do it.

Website and App TLC

But suppose you're not into burgers. Let's ask you about your website instead. When did you last update it? If you are like most, you built it, or had someone build it for you, and that's that. But a static website, at worst, is out of date, so that prices and specifications are wrong, future events have already occurred, and any *news* is old hat. Obviously if your site is like that, no potential customer browsing would ever have reason to come back and will instead devote current attention—and most likely their next order—to a more interesting shop window—someone else's. *Your website is your best shop window*—one that works tirelessly for you. Surely shouldn't you support it with a little TLC from time to time?

You must remember the time when a prospect called you and seconds into the conversation they said "Can I see it on your website?" and your answer was "Err" and the prospective sale was lost. Unless there are trade secrets, make everything available online. Even then, when referring to a secret, give a mechanism for finding out: for example, *For details call sales on 1-800-XXX-XXXX*. That way your tireless helper (i.e., the website) is being more informative to prospects out there than even you. You can't remember every fact about everything, but it can. And unlike you, it does it without protest 24/7.

And another thing: We are now in a world where a website alone is no longer giving you the digital presence to match that of your competitors. There are plenty of tools available to enhance the chances of your website being found—generically called Search Engine Optimization (SEO). You should go and find them and use them. How else do you think your competitors appear higher up on Google than your business?

Maybe you do it the same way they do. Buy keywords. That is pay Google (and the other search engines of this world) every time someone searches on words that lead to your site being located. When you explore this opportunity as a keyword buyer, you will find the same chaos as you do if you search yourself for something. Typing in *widgets* might bring hundreds of thousands of results. Who is first in the listings? Probably the industry leader who will have paid more than anyone else for that billing. More modestly, we could perhaps pay for the two keywords together of *fluorescent widgets*? Then if someone searches on those two words, your website might be the first they discover and we know that *fluorescent* is relevant to them in any subsequent transaction.

Clearly the more specialized the word(s), the fewer responses but also usually much cheaper and, as we have already said, *relevant*.

Even with all this, the website is just a beginning. These days, to reach people across the web there are other games to play. Do you have a Facebook site? Are you on Instagram? Do you Tweet? Beyond that, have you got an App? Can your customer find your app on their smartphone, and with a single click, reorder their previous purchase?

If any of these concepts are alien to you, go find someone of a younger generation to explain them to you. Possibly better and done by a number of folks we know, have that younger person within your family actually manage all your social media—as this branch of advertising is known—in return for their weekly allowance/pocket money. You should explain to them this is a win/win/win. Triple wins are rare animals, but here you get your business a shiny and changing media presence that can only help you move forward. The youngster gets (presumably) an increased allowance for simply playing on the computer. Finally, and again important in this day and age, the youngster also gets to put Social Media Manager on their first resume, which must boost their ultimate career prospects.

> This is only a short comment, but we cannot stress how important the appropriate use of social media is—so make it happen for you and your widgets. If there is one certainty in life, it is that the Internet is not going away any time soon—but to make impact, you must use it wisely.

Pause: Did you make notes of things in the Action This Today section in the back of this book? If not, please take this opportunity to review the prior pages to identify again any thoughts and ideas you want to follow up on.

CHAPTER 16

Change: *How about...*the Price Model?

Subscription?

Have you noticed that the most expensive (hidden) element of your cost structure is probably the cost of customer acquisition, that is, the cost of getting new customers or getting existing customers to come back and spend again. Here are a few pointers to what you might do:

- Increase the price point.
- Increase the amount of money each customer spends at each transaction (volume of purchases).
- Increase the frequency of purchase (every week, every month).
- Make it easier to stay buying from you longer (before they go looking elsewhere).

Each of these levers, either applied individually or in combination, will vastly improve the returns you get from the dollars you spend to win these customers in the first place—this will release immense energy for growth.

Additionally, if your business finds itself with idle staff when the frequency of customers visits changes, then you might want to significantly change your pricing structure toward subscriptions. But we suspect you might not think of your business as a subscription business. We never thought of gentleman's barbers as a subscription business model, until we became a loyal customers a year ago!

Imagine if you have a chain of hairdressers, beauty spa, nail spa, massage parlors, and so on and your business relies on customers coming back multiple times in the year. Can you redesign your price from being a price per visit to a price per month or per quarter with unlimited (within reason) visits within that time period? If the price is based on a per-visit basis, then we might only get our hair cut, when we notice our hair is getting unruly. But if we have signed up for a monthly price of say $80, paid monthly or maybe further discounted for quarterly or annually, we might be tempted to come as frequently as our weekly timetables allow. Illustratively, instead of paying $45/visit, and where we might get round to visiting once or twice a month, if we pay in advance, and can come weekly, then the price per visit becomes $20. Let's further review the pros and cons from the consumers' perspective and for your business:

Pros for us:

- Cheaper per visit cost.
- We look groomed all the time.
- We can build a weekly pattern, and the whole scheduling is much easier.
- We can get into a habit with the same hairdresser each visit.
- Each haircut is more efficient, and doesn't take as long.

Pros for the business:

- Although less price, per visit, greater annual fee from each client.
- Staff are less idle, so their time flies by.
- Staff's income doesn't fluctuate so much.
- Each haircut is more efficient, and doesn't take as long.
- Tips from customers go up as the customers don't feel the impact of the payment on each visit.
- Customers that visit weekly are more likely to refer new clients, further reducing the cost of customer acquisition.
- Increased customer loyalty.

And perhaps best of all, a number will keep paying and not visit at all—remember all those people with unused gym memberships you know.

Deep Discount

Are you using a discount coupon type of promotion as your marketing tool? There are many marketing companies who will approach prospective customers for you on their own databases, persuading them to try you by offering a coupon for a deep discount off your usual price. Be warned: 60 percent off your regular price is not unheard of, and of the remaining 40 percent, half might go to the marketing company, leaving you with perhaps only 20 percent of usual price.

But it is not all doom and gloom. Once these prospective clients have tried you, and enjoyed your service or product, they'll want to come back and pay the normal price. To make sure they do, show them the advantages of signing up for a subscription. If you follow our hairdressing numbers, the subscription could still appear as deep discount from the one off price, but benefit your business as above.

If you have any business where each incremental customer doesn't add any additional costs to your business (within reason), for example, a yoga class, or in fact almost any type of class, then this is an absolute no-brainer.

Pause: Did you make notes of things in the Action This Today section in the back of this book? If not, please take this opportunity to review the prior pages to identify again any thoughts and ideas you want to follow up on.

CHAPTER 17

Change: *How about...* Money Matters?

Leverage Other Funding

Some of these *utility bill* leeches (that we referenced in the money section) have become even more sophisticated of late and apply many of the same principles—notably taking a share of what you save/make—and offer their talents *to apply for grants for you*. Some are prepared to assist you in taking advantage of government or regional grants. Why not get one of these fish in (are leeches fish?) and get them to tell you without obligation what is available, whether they think it might work for you, and if so how much they'll charge as a success fee? If it can apply to you and there are many potential schemes out there, with backdated claims and all, you could be due a tidy sum.

You do of course also have government loan finance—be it for regional policy, employment, exports, and so on. And if you had one a while back, are you eligible to return to the trough for another, or more? How imaginative is your bank in financing? Since you last met with the bank, does it now have offerings of inventory or asset finance schemes that could help you that you are currently unaware of?

Remember, there is a maxim that a bank will only lend to someone who can prove they don't need the money. It has to be substantially true, or interest charged on loans would be sky-high. One way for the bank to feel more secure is for it to seek a personal guarantee from you as further security for an advance. Please resist, because if your business fails, you are not then going to be able to repay the loan yourself because you've lost your employment (as well as the business) and the whole thing gets very messy.

Pause: Did you make notes of things in the Action This Today section in the back of this book? If not, please take this opportunity to review the prior pages to identify again any thoughts and ideas you want to follow up on.

CHAPTER 18

Change: *How about...*the Process?

Change the Process

Suppose you're a business that needs local people to do the work, like a pest control business, a landscaping business, window washing, or any such people-intensive, yet local business. You've grown phenomenally in your home city and now are doing the same again in another city. Yet, once you left the original operation running under the watchful eye of your trusted lieutenant and you embarked on tackling the new city, you find it's not working as smoothly. It should be because this time you've set the new region up in a way that is easier for you to set it up, and therefore want to move on eventually to city #3, and so forth. You've hired numerous people, none are like your trusted lieutenant in your home city—but you know that, you're not expecting that. Nonetheless you have hoped that you will find someone entrepreneurial enough so you can leave this operation in their capable hands. But these people just aren't settling in. What's going on?

Finding people that are hardworking *and* entrepreneurial, *and* willing to work to *your* formula is very tough indeed. Let's look at what you're expecting these people to do. You're expecting them to win over new customers, each time they go visit a new home. Then you are expecting them to "do the work." Then collect the money. And follow up. All on your formula, yet in their perception, they're doing all the hard work themselves, so why are you the boss? And being entrepreneurial themselves, they can see there's an opportunity to do this all for themselves and cut you out of the loop altogether.

So how can you do things differently? Remove some of the *and*s from the above description of their role. Any ideas? One way would be to change the processes and split the roles of finding customers, doing work, and collecting money, so that you centrally do the customer acquisition, customer relationship, payment collection, and follow up. So that the only task you are expecting your workers to do is the work itself, for which they will get paid. And if you feel they are instrumental in winning the client over in the first visit, then maybe offer a commission for each new client signed up.

We know this will feel like a big departure from the model you used in your home city, where you were able to hand over to a lieutenant all of your established daily routines. The point being, when your ambition changed, and you decided to set up city #2 and so forth, you needed to make a huge change to your business operation. If you didn't make fundamental changes to the components of the business, the growth you desire may leave you stuck back on the plateau or, worse, city #2 may be an abject failure.

Don't Make or Buy?

Throughout personal and business life, one has to constantly make decisions. In fact, it is never as simple as make or buy. There is a third dimension: *ignore*.

We raise the possibility to ignore here because it is really powerful and all too infrequently engaged. Why is it that when you appear to reach the fork in the road, one always feels it has to be "we do this ourselves" or "we have others do it for us" as the only choices? What, pray tell, is the cost of *doing nothing at all*?

People are often in this third category. Someone in your business will scream and shout about needing an additional member of staff. The need will appear so urgent that you have to acquire this person fully trained via an agency, right now. Clearly that's the *buy* option. Agency fees will be pricey—and if they're not, you are simply paying someone significant sums to trawl resumes from the Internet. This new staff member will be pricey, and it might be six months before you or they discover it was a mis-hire and you go through the whole process again. The *make* option is to take an untrained (in this arena) person from elsewhere in your business and let them grow into the role. This might be an option for a Legacy Person—you remember, someone acquired a while back but who you now only pay JIC. But, the third option, you could choose to do nothing at all.

The vacuum of this third option will, however, incur the displeasure of the person requesting the hire unless ameliorated in some way. The first way is to remind them who the boss is, whose money is funding his or her wages, and so on. The second way is to go for a little shared blame allocation, that is, "we can't afford it." But the best approach for all is to look at this as a catalyst for a process review. Whilst we can hear you say "this is not doing nothing," the outcome certainly is.

Narrowly, a process review would look at the job seeking to be filled and simply to see if it can be eliminated. However, simple common sense would also include a look both upstream and downstream in the work flow leading to/from this appointment to see if the process can be made leaner and more efficient. Don't make the common mistake of stopping this enquiry at the boundary walls between departments or activities. It might be a change elsewhere—may be demolishing a boundary wall or even soliciting a change inside a supplier company of yours—can render this post (or another) redundant.

Would you repaint (or hire someone to paint) your garden fence if you were going to demolish it in another month and plant a row of conifers instead? No, of course you wouldn't. "Ignore" has its rightful place in the "make or buy" decision tree.

Do You Make or Buy?

When Britain was still great, it was the workshop of the world. Cotton was brought to England to be spun on machines made in England and operated in England, so that it could export cotton-based textiles worldwide. Giant railway works existed in Britain so it could make steam trains from scratch and send them worldwide—perhaps to further the collection of cotton and the distribution of wares. Even the steel for the Sydney Harbour Bridge in Australia was made in England, half a world away from its intended place of use.

But almost none of this happens today. Machines made by Germans, Japanese, and Chinese are now sent to remote and poor countries to manufacture cotton garments a few cents cheaper than anywhere else for us to buy in our local shopping malls. And when did you last hear of any country exporting a railway engine, steam, or otherwise? In pure Adam Smith economic speak, his laws of comparative and absolute advantage have been taken, used, and abused to the *n*th degree.

> Are you following the same rules with your business? You buy coffee in for the staff to consume; you don't try to grow the beans yourself. You buy the instruction books you pack with your widgets from a printer—there's no Thomas Caxton in you. So why do you even make the widgets yourself?

We have to ask, because only when you are being truthful with yourself can we discuss make or buy, properly.

Now, it could be the reason was historic and over time that reason has disappeared. In that case, doing it now because you always have is probably as close to Lemming-like leap off a cliff mentality as we are going to find. *Wake up!*

Could it be a very real reason that you're based here, and not in some far off, efficient, production center, because you can't stand foreign food? *Wake up!*

Could it be that you're making your product here because you have to be, because your customers are here? Plausible if you're selling freshly cooked pizza or ready-mixed concrete or legally necessary if your key contract(s) demand it, but these reasons in practice cover very few real situations.

Truth is (probably) you are still making widgets only because you haven't sensibly explored *not* making them yourself! We'll take that as a fact, and on that basis there is no point in going through all the subprocesses you undertake to see to what extent these can be bought in (if physical) or outsourced (if otherwise) at a lower total cost than taking the do-it-all-yourself approach?

Just promise us, as you go away and ponder this, you remember that when comparing make or buy, you are fairly charging the make option with its full share of overheads. Not just the rent for the floor space the machine sits on, but also the space taken up by its raw material in store.

Not just the staff costs of those who work the machine but their share of the office people (who pay their wages, order the materials, you, etc.) and the office costs like the coffee, the factory cleaning, and so on. We haven't finished yet. Have you allowed for the time when the machine is idle due to not being used 24/7 × 52 weeks? The cost of the machine itself and any repairs or servicing?

Taken to extreme, if you bought everything rather than made anything, there'd be no need for HR, accountants, premises, equipment, vehicles, and so on. Indeed, you could jump out of the loop altogether and simply license someone else to make your widgets for delivery to your customers. Then you could be on a tropical island (assuming the weather, scenery, and food were to your liking) just banking the license fees. Tempting, isn't it?

OK, we were a little harsh on you. Maybe you are making the widgets because you truly have some proprietary method (other assets) that gives you an advantage in the making, in which case you should be doing the reverse of the above, and offering your lesser known competitors the chance to outsource their production to you. Why? To allow them to focus on a different value add, maybe in a different geography or with other complementary products. Making their life a little easier for them, and improving your own strength in your industry.

Leverage Your #1 Asset

Mostly in this book we have considered your business as a single entity. That makes sense—the *all for one, one for all* is how a business works. But maybe the changes you want to make are around a single asset—your most valuable asset—which hitherto is underemployed. Let's park widgets for a moment and think of a few other examples.

A pizza restaurant chain—you have fancy pizza ovens and great evening trade—but what to do in the day time? How about pizza-making classes? Hold classes for adults who'll doubtless buy wine from you whilst learning. Likewise holding classes for kids, who will certainly bring accompanying adults (see wine) and want soft drinks and ice creams as well as a ticket to the class. And why sell tickets to the class one at a time? Instead, how about you offer the class as a birthday party package? And if they've learned, they'll want to be able to make them for themselves.

So why not sell them the tools, pizza mix, and other nonperishable ingredients? You could even consider a subscription pizza service.

Do you own a 24/7 gas station? Why not become a parcel collection/delivery point for your locality making it easier for your outworking neighborhood to get their Internet purchases? Earn fees from the Internet company or your patrons, who doubtless will become more loyal to your gas pumps too. Install electric points and you gain more friends, who may well buy coffee and doughnuts from you whilst their car feeds itself outside.

As a veterinarian practice, why not stock the large packs (we're thinking 10- to 28-lb sizes) of your recommended dog food for sale to your clients? You know their car is outside—they've just brought their dog in it. You know they are focused on the animal's well-being, have their credit card to hand, and are not minded to do price comparison or Internet shopping at *your* point of sale.

As a trades business, be it a gardening, decorating, plumbing, electrical, visiting people's homes, why not develop an (annual) peace-of-mind service call and *sell it* as part of wrapping up whichever task put your business in front of the customer? That gives you an opportunity to contact the customer again any time after say nine months and make the service appointment timing to help fill your quiet spots.

Back with widgets. Why not approach your best customers and find out what, outside of widgets, they find painful to buy or build themselves and offer to be an outsource supplier of them? This might achieve better utilization of your people and equipment and of course, the deeper you are in with your customer, the less likely they will want to sever the relationship sometime in the future.

> Have you noticed the common theme here? Whilst making better use of your most valuable asset, you are creating a better, deeper relationship with your clients/customers/patients, and so on, without necessarily adding to them numerically. And you are selling them more, getting a greater share of their wallet.

Pause: Did you make notes of things in the Action This Today section in the back of this book? If not, please take this opportunity to review the prior pages to identify again any thoughts and ideas you want to follow up on.

CHAPTER 19

Change: *How about...* Other Stuff?

Change, change, change. Few people embrace change naturally—it is outside their comfort zone, but hopefully not yours. How many times have you said to yourself *everything changes* but forgot to include your own business in that statement? As authors, we hope that some of the changes above are changes you are already beginning to embrace. Don't stop, life is a constant change.

As a business owner and entrepreneur you are very attuned to changes outside your business, attuned to the needs of your customers changing, attuned to understanding your staff, attuned to everything. But we also know that you have worked very hard over the past few years making your business efficient. And in making it efficient—to your own particular way of knowing what works—you have probably allowed yourself to fall into the trap of wanting to keep things within your business from change. Our job here, as we help you break through your business's glass ceiling, is to once again remind you to catalyze more change into things you have yourself settled into a rhythm.

And now, if you want to put your foot on the accelerator, turn the page to see Grow, coming next...

Pause: Did you make notes of things in the Action This Today section in the back of this book? If not, please take this opportunity to review the prior pages to identify again any thoughts and ideas you want to follow up on.

CHAPTER 20

To Grow from Here *Try This...*

Have You Banked the Resources from STOP?

There are three reasons why growth is illusive for Plateau Businesses. The first reason is the lack of resources, which the first two sections of the book so far have been dedicated to. There's literally thousands of tactics you can deploy to grow your business. Hundreds of books, websites, and blogs are dedicated to this topic. You're probably already familiar with many of them. However, for Plateau Businesses, those tactics are mostly redundant as those tactics are resource hungry—like money and energy—that is, until you've recovered and banked time, money, resources, energy, and focus from our earlier Stop initiatives. The second reason is beautifully explained by the late Peter Drucker who said "We spend a lot of time teaching leaders what to do. We don't spend enough time teaching leaders what to stop. Half the leaders I have met don't need to learn what to do. They need to learn what to stop."

Make the Plateau Busters *Yours*

The final reason for illusiveness of growth is trying ideas that may have worked elsewhere, but don't work for you now.

As you read on, don't oppose our *Try this* ideas. We have captured the ideas here—not necessarily as precise solutions for you to challenge or critique, but as parables to encourage you to find the parallels in your business. Your curiosity around your own thoughts will lead to ideas that will grow your business. We are interested in you implementing your ideas that come to your mind as your curiosity is sparked by what you read here. In other words, the Plateau Busters that are most likely to succeed are those that *you* devise inspired by what you read. We'll call them *your Plateau Busters*.

Try This...New Customers through New Hires

What is the next natural step-change in your business: 20 percent more or 200 percent more over the next 5 years?

But wait...did you free up the time, money, resources, energy, and focus in earlier sections of this book to truly enable growth? If not, you're not going to get the Plateau Buster growth you promised yourself. You're really only going to tinker at the edges. So is that what you want? If not, please go to the back of this book, and take action on the notes you already made.

OK, so you did take action, already. Great, so now you are resourced to grow. You should have people capable of more or at least people able to manage more people—without simply becoming pen-pushers—when the volumes increase. You may still need to ask yourself: Are the premises large enough, and do you have enough equipment to make more? Are there other operational constraints?

If you can easily produce 20 percent more widgets, will your existing customers take them?

Of course not! Because if they could buy more, you already would be selling more, wouldn't you? So, you will need more customers, probably beyond those gained with your 80/20 clear out in an earlier section. Should you think about hiring a new customer acquisition person, as it is probably you who still does all the selling?

If your widgets are on message and of their time, it would be possible to hire someone to start tele-selling them for you. It's a fairly thankless task as they will undoubtedly be frustrated in trying to reach buyers inside organizations, and when they have reached the one with the order pad, more likely than not, they will be rebuffed. Nonetheless if they throw enough mud, some might stick and the person you engage will probably welcome a low basic with a significant commission incentive for new sales. And, don't forget, do also let them try out on some of the customers you have lost over time—no, not the bad payers, but the defectors.

If, however, your widgets are mature items bought by mature buyers, you probably need a mature salesman (like yourself) to sell face to face. Great salesmen pick the companies they work for based on their own assessments of product and opportunities. They don't respond to adverts.

Salesmen hired via an advert is clearly not succeeding where they are (or were). They ask for big basics and guaranteed commission to cover the long period before they succeed or, as is more likely, you lose patience with them. So our advice is not to use this route. Instead consider a variation on the above model—hire a former senior person of a rival supplier or substantial customer who is otherwise retired. They don't want to work full time and therefore pay is not the only factor. They want to feel they are achieving something rather than sitting on their backsides. However, they don't want to be deeply involved in the nitty gritty, and that overhead will fall back on you. What they really are is a rolodex of active buyers to whom they can open doors you never could.

Few senior people hired in such consulting capacities stay more than a year with any business—but in that year, their who's who is yours for the plundering and of course, once exploited, you would hope to keep the customers much longer than the consultant.

To gain one, you need to be proactive, go gamekeeper-turned poacher, and seek to hire someone selling into you (or against you) who impresses. They will be expensive, but suitably motivated, generate sales that will lift your heart (and wallet).

An important footnote is these guys often also want a chunk of the ownership of your business as motivation. In our experience, any agreement should be in the form of share options which should vest over, say, a three-year period and disappear if they are no longer working with you. And if share options and vest are strange notions to you, get your lawyer to draw up an agreement. But whatever happens—no handshake deals—make sure it is all in writing.

Writing doesn't necessarily have to mean an expensive trip to the lawyers. The chances are the document will be agreed, both parties will sign it, and it stays in a drawer until is ultimately redundant. But it must be unambiguous and attempt to foresee obvious potential future problems. And the web is full of templates and examples of almost every conceivable document—as we previously identified—so why reinvent the wheel when some or fewer dollars will do the work for you?

If widgets is not your game, how about an extra sales person to extend your hours? A waiter/waitress and a chef could give you a breakfast shift in each of your restaurants that you didn't have before. A trainee veterinarian could be hired to do routine injections and medications beyond the hours you want to work yourself. As a landscaper, you could usefully employ someone to hand out fliers around the neighborhood of your last piece of work, showing what you have just completed.

Alternatively, if your service business is maybe a five-location tuition center spread across a major metropolitan city that relies on word of mouth for new students, then perhaps you ought to hire a part-time digital influencing person to extend your reach.

Try This...New Customers—Internationally

We suspect you are doing a trivial amount of overseas business with a buyer who found you rather than the other way around. The export market for widgets is huge. There are only two important barriers to you doing more international business: language and being paid.

You can export more than widgets. One of the authors worked with a university urologist professor to develop a computer program providing easy-to-read urinary analysis reports for a bioscience company. The professor later attending an international symposium mentioned the program and, hey presto! The author received an export order for the same software from 3,500 miles away—two sales, one piece of work. Can this become a repeatable channel?

Dealing with language, it is important you appoint an agent. The agent should be based in one of your intended markets and it is he/they who will be able to tell you what local regulations you will need to adhere to rather than you seeking to learn all the foreign regulations yourself. They will also be able to make suggestions for your product's presentation to be attractive to local customers. Most important, they will open doors to prospective customers. It won't stop you having to travel to meet prospects, but a good agent will use a block of your time to meet many prospects at one time rather than you making many separate single journeys. And of course they speak the local language.

As for being paid, you already know how hard it is to collect from domestic customers. Put in geographical separation, time difference, and possibly a language barrier and you might as well be trading with the moon. Many companies overseas are honorable and stick to trade terms and pay promptly, but there are equally any number who play on the remoteness from you and will allow your ignorance or lack of tenacity to overcome the distance and language differences to only ever pay your bill when they want more product. Our favorite way of dealing with this is to have two columns on your international price list: the price you actually want to achieve as a *Cash with order price* and marked up by 10 percent as the *trade price*. Only a fool, or a penniless customer, would go for the latter.

Finally, be very sure of both your customer's terms of business and their country's rules too. Many buyers expect to be able to *and in practice do* take payment discounts even when paying according to your terms and a lot of countries (particularly in Asia) like to take some withholding tax from any money remitted overseas. Then of course there is the exchange risk and the bank charges deducted by both the remitter's bank and yours.

If you know what to expect from the deals you are going to be doing, you can price accordingly.

Try This...Let Others Do It

Licensing is the methodology of using a paper agreement to let someone else do something with your design and rewarding you for it.

Before you read on, take another gulp of air and promise not to say no to this or indeed any of this before you have looked at these opportunities with a fresh pair of eyes and genuine curiosity. And if your eyes are tired and jaded, how about a genuine fresh pair from a trusted friend?

That agreed, come back to the question: Why do you make widgets at all? Could you simply buy someone else's, with a little smart packaging—done by the manufacturer on your behalf—sell them to your customers, and make a profit—without any infrastructure of your own, at all? And if you can, is that better than continuing with the hassle that caused you to buy this book in the first place?

Or could you pass your infrastructure together with a robust licensing agreement to some other country's manufacturer who, with lower costs, can make them cheaper than you, both for you to supply to your customers and for them to supply to some of their own and to pay you a license fee on those latter sales?

Or finally, could you find a manufacturer in an appropriate piece of geography to manufacture in addition to you—both then to supply local markets of your customers? That may well be a better thing to do than for you to try and establish your own additional plant in a country you don't properly understand, where the language is not familiar, and you have little chance of effective supervision—without giving up the day job.

Pause: Did you make notes of things in the Action This Today section in the back of this book? If not, please take this opportunity to review the prior pages to identify again any thoughts and ideas you want to follow up on.

CHAPTER 21

To Grow *Try This...*
Delegation and Controls

Scarily everything you have read so far is but a warm-up to the main event of *Delegation and Controls* and what leads from that delegation. Getting that right is everything that stands between you and a bigger, brighter future.

We want to help you make some foundational changes in your business that will set you up for identifying and then implementing the growth opportunities—*your* Plateau Busters! This section may at first seem somewhat radical, but once you put some of these suggestions into action, you will probably be impressed with how they work for you. And yes, it's all your work, we are merely shining light on the paths ahead and guiding you toward the best of those paths available to you. You will need to do all of the hard work of this journey to the next level on your organization's growth trajectory.

We asked you a few pages ago: "*What is the next natural step-change in your business: 20 percent more or 200 percent more over the next 5 years?*" We also asked you near the beginning of this book: "*What your greatest asset is?*"

We suspect you, yourself, might be the greatest asset, and invariably if you intend to grow, and particularly if you go for the more aggressive growth ambition, you'll need to consider your span of control. We human beings seem to wrongly think control and chaos are opposites—such that if you let go of control, it will be chaos.

Try This...Grow Span of Control

It can simply be that you don't want to let go. Let's not label you as a control freak because you're not. Let's instead recognize that actually it's your money in play and you should rightfully be connected overwhelmingly with decisions to be made with it. Or is it? Do you have other shareholders and, if so, are their interests best served by your unwillingness to delegate? Because that's what it amounts to—a business ceiling imposed by the maximum span of control you can (or at least seek to) exercise. You run a tight ship because…

We need control in our lives because nobody likes to pay for something they haven't had. A restaurant check with an extra dish or bottle of wine either not ordered or never received is sent back with annoyance. Annoyance of it having to be checked and found wanting, annoyance that it is a less than perfect end to what should have been an enjoyable occasion.

With that simple thought in mind, we would guess, in your business, if it is like almost all others, cash is not in bountiful supply and therefore you like to make sure only correct purchase invoices are paid and so on. We imagine you operationally do this because it is still you that cut the checks or at least signs them if you are not already doing similarly electronically.

So how do you know they are correct? Our guess is you look at the invoice and think "Oh yes, I remember that batch of widget castings being delivered." And therein lies the problem.

How can you begin to expand the business if you have to witness every delivery? But of course you don't. We are guessing, for instance, you don't read the utility meters yourself and that you also accept what the Telco tells you are your business' usage charges for the previous month. So why not delegate the task of watching every incoming delivery and have a control mechanism in place so you know remotely what has happened?

Give the person nearest the receiving bay a rubber stamp—or the electronic equivalent—that says *Received and checked*…and ask that they apply the stamp and their signature to every delivery note received. Then come payment time, pay invoices with matching-stamped delivery notes and query the ones without. It should go without saying that the task is not simply signing their name, but to check that the goods delivered agree with the documentation and that their signature is evidence of that fact.

So suddenly you have delegated a responsibility and installed a control to make sure it happens. Whilst with any delegation there is a risk of short-cutting or cheating, the signatory will know their job is dependent on doing this and not be found wanting. And in any event, until you are a much larger organization, you are almost certainly going to observe this operative performing this task from time to time—probably because you will find yourself in the receiving area from time to time on some other mission.

If you can do it for deliveries, you can do it for sales. In fact, you probably do already. Somebody, and it's not you, already ticks off each customer's packing list so that what is dispatched from your premises matches what you bill the customer for. Depending on values and complexity, you might well have separate pickers of customer orders (from your warehouse) and packers who check the order as part of preparing it for dispatch. Initials on internal paperwork will confirm these actions and by whom.

The chances are, notwithstanding our earlier suggestions about hiring salespeople, is it still *you* who handles all the new sales enquiries? Is that really about personal service, only you with the required knowledge and only you who can make key pricing decisions or again is it simply that you have not delegated some of this? Why not define the rules (= control) and allow other people to handle some of the sales enquiries? The rules can set maximum discounts, credit checking, the contact cycle, and follow-up, and the exceptional criteria where sales leads *must* be referred to you.

Certainly, the discipline of following up on an enquiry—say a first reply within one hour, the offering of online or physical sales collateral, booking a sales appointment, further follow-up calls to a longer timescale—is, in all honesty, better done by someone else. Someone who doesn't have all the other issues you have in front of you every day that stop *you* sticking to *your rules*. To do that effectively, the delegatee will need to maintain a log of activities and hey! Suddenly you have a control tool too.

If you are worried your salesperson is going to give each new enquiry maximum discount, the choice is yours. Either make them refer each enquiry to you and duplicate the manpower involved, or make part of their remuneration a commission based on margin. The latter will ensure they are as keen as you are that proper pricing is upheld.

Try This...Develop Accountable Catchers

Throwing a ball at people who can't catch results in a lot of balls on the floor. You probably still have some balls on the floor from the last time you tried to delegate in a meaningful way. This time it will be different as you'll also develop your team's catching skills—by that we mean accountability.

If accountability is dropping in your workplace, it's likely because people are being underchallenged. You may be delegating less and less from a concern that employees' jobs are too big? Reverse this and delegate more to develop your employees but at the same time provide feedback and mentoring.

Resist the urge to protect people from natural consequences. People's choices and the consequences should be made visible and undiluted without drama. After an employee gets data from reality, you can be ready to jump in with factual feedback and assistance with corrective action, if needed.

Provide feedback, as factually and unemotionally as possible. Just a few sentences. If the feedback goes beyond a simple observation of the facts, you're going to invoke the employee's ego, which in turn encourages self-defensiveness, resistance, and blaming others.

Feedback short, self-reflection long. Briefly report what you see, and quickly hand over responsibility for self-reflection and associated improvement to whom it belongs to—the employee.

Then add an assignment to prompt this action—see questions below—and set a date for a future conversation about what the employee discovers. The key focus is not the feedback, but for you to inspire self-reflection.

Self-reflection comes from a place of seeking truth, leading to inner discovery rather than trying to force it through external pressure from you or others. You can fuel this through great questions and simple assignments. Suggested paired reflection questions look like:

- What are the facts?
- What would *great* look like in this situation?
- What helped?
- What hindered results?
- What was your part in this outcome?
- What might you do to add value here next time?

Corroborate self-reflection. After all this self-reflection, the employee will be tempted to find a colleague to verify their situation—maybe seeking an empathetic ear. Ideally that supportive ear needs to have been through this approach beforehand and thus not allow self-pity or drama—just the facts. Soon, your pool of employees that have experienced this process will demonstrate accountability themselves and encourage their colleagues toward the same.

Try This...Vacation

Vacation time is precious, that's why you plan it out in some detail—an investment in your time to ensure when the vacation arrives you make the best use of *that* time. But there's no point in planning a vacation that you can't take—because the business is too important and needs your constant attendance.

Wrong! Wrong for so many reasons. If the business is going to collapse because of a short absence on your part, it can't be much of a business. Ponder this for a second, because should you to want to sell it, the truth is there's no business without you, and therefore no likelihood of a sale.

If you have delegated, if you have installed some controls, then the business can be on autopilot and you should be able to vacation at any time and for as long as you want. Getting to that stage does require two things—extra effort on your part and trust.

The extra effort is the work involved in setting up the controls around delegation and helping your employees become accountable. The next piece of the jigsaw here is about overcoming your fear of letting go.

Think about it. How much more effort is it to set up a system—equals control and accountability—as opposed to all the briefings and notes you would have to give and make anyway for your staff if you were going to go away for a planned week or two off? And of course with systems in place, your next absence after this one is already catered for.

The prospect of a vacation could be the stimulus you need to begin this process. Start on the delegation route today as a test. You are still on site, so you can monitor the effect of any delegation, related controls, and accountability, making changes if necessary. When tuned and you are happy that it works well with you present, then we think there is a sporting chance it will work well when you are on that long overdue vacation.

This happened in a coffee business one of the authors was involved in. The owner, happy the controls were working, announced a faraway vacation for himself. He refused to give any contact details, telling the staff they had the tools, authority, and importantly competence to deal with anything that might arise in his absence! "But what if the place burns down?" queried one. "I'm sure you'll deal with it," replied the owner.

It didn't burn.

And there is a valuable side-effect. Staff can react very positively to the award of responsibility, in terms of personal esteem but also in their commitment to your business—someone else who cares about your business—as promised in the first paragraph of *stop-what if…it's your people?* A true win–win.

Try This…Captain in Charge?

Ever been on a cruise ship? The two expected answers are yes and not yet. But you know the form because even if not yet, you've seen the movies, adverts, and documentaries. Here we are discussing food service on board. We'd all like to think the chef and maître d' sit down the night before and plan the next day's dining room menus. But wrong! They are determined months ahead in head office. The same place determines portion size and anticipates guest numbers, and clever computers guess what the guests will choose from the menus. This allows supplies to be ordered in the right quantities and delivered to the right dock on the right day, way ahead of time.

At dockside, the actual delivery is matched to the order by the food and beverage controller, who on board is the one who issues the anticipated number of steaks and so on to the chef—who naturally signs for them. Later the same controller looks at plates coming back from the dining room to see what's been left by the guests. Clearly if not there, the food has been enjoyed, whilst if still there in quantity, the controller will tell head office and have the computer in the future switch broccoli for asparagus and so on.

OK, you are not running a cruise ship. But you are forward planning, you are seeking to avoid waste, and we hope you are reacting to customer feedback. You will also see from the above illustration that the captain of the ship has nothing to do with the whole process—it is delegated and controlled for him. So why is this not the same for you? If what you do has a method, delegate someone to run it. Ensure there are controls so that if for instance a vital component is running out, an alert mechanism doesn't just report that to you, but also efficiently reorders it without your intervention. It should also tell you about the reorder—then you can sleep more peacefully at night. But in both cases it is to tell you, not ask you, otherwise much of the efficiency is lost.

Please pause here for a moment. We bet there's a long list of questions you are currently asked in your business. Which of these, after appropriate training and putting systems in place, could be mere FYI updates to you, versus still requiring an answer from you, as they do at present?

Beware though of customer feedback, not received directly. In a software company, one of the authors received feedback only via the sales director. According to the director, there was a lot of demand for new features X, Y, and Z and all the prospects were holding off for feature W. When challenged, *a lot* was one prospect and *all* was two!

Pause: Did you make notes of things in the Action This Today section in the back of this book? If not, please take this opportunity to review the prior pages to identify again any thoughts and ideas you want to follow up on.

CHAPTER 22

To Grow *Try This*…Do the Right Things Now

Now that you've delegated with controls, you're probably still a tad nervous about the potential for chaos. We would be too!

It's tempting for leaders to assign goals to motivate their employees and curb the risk of chaos.

Try This…Go beyond Goals

You've probably become accustomed to creating goals that are based on numbers and goals that are SMART (Specific, Measurable, Assignable, Realistic, Time based). Contrary to our earlier promise we are indulging in some business school acronyms as you're probably familiar with SMART goals. We admit that simple goals like monthly sales targets or hourly widget production forecasts fit the SMART template. However, when trying to imbed a game-changer growth culture in our teams, developing SMART goals for major change creates problems.

A recent *Harvard Business Review* (HBR) article titled "Goals Gone Wild" gave an explicit warning:

> Goals may cause systematic problems in organizations due to narrowed focus, unethical behavior, increased risk taking, decreased cooperation and decreased intrinsic motivation. Use care when applying goals to your organization.

That warning is relevant to what we are saying here because, in our opinion, when leaders try to share major goals with others in their organization, the recipients are unlikely to experience the power of the goals in the way the leader intends, often resulting in one or more of the negative outcomes identified in the HBR warning. Employees are typically left with questions: *How does this change what I do day to day, other than somehow, I am expected to work harder to achieve more, without additional resources, within the same number of hours in the day?* So let's go beyond goals.

If you're still not yet convinced, recall, from your memory banks, news (which emerged around September 2016) about 3.5 million fake bank accounts that had been opened without customers' permission between 2009 and 2016. In March 2019, *New York Times* reported that

> At the heart of its rehabilitation efforts, Wells Fargo said, it has changed how it motivates employees. No longer will they be individually rewarded for reaching sales targets, or punished for falling short. Branch workers were told that their primary job is to serve customers, not sell them things.

*Try This…*Go beyond a Strategic Plan

Like goals, a strategic plan seems very good to the originators, who have toiled for weeks and months to build it, to steer the business in a new direction. It's tempting for leaders to share the strategic plans to motivate their employees and curb the risk of chaos.

Yet to the recipients, it's often a murky document that rarely answers the inevitable question: *How does this change what I do day to day, other than somehow I am expected to work harder to achieve more, without additional resources, within the same number of hours in the day?* The strategic plan then becomes less relevant as time passes, and the plan starts to expire.

> I have no use whatsoever for projections or forecasts. They create an illusion of apparent precision. The more meticulous they are, the more concerned you should be
>
> —Warren Buffet

Instead, your employees need something that lets them take responsibility for their actions as you delegate more to them. Something that helps your team control their own behavior, knowing they are *walking the walk.*

Something that allows the employees to know what they need to do differently, know how they need to behave on a day-to-day basis.

Strategic plans and strategic goals are useful for you and your senior management team in how you allocate your capital and how you might re-engineer your organization. But when it comes to motivating the wider employees, what we need is something to complement the goals, to complement strategic plans.

Try This...Doing the Right Things, NOW

How else to motivate your people? As a Plateau Business—much like any sports team that is going through a difficult patch—you don't have the feel-good factor that motivates people, that comes with being a start-up or growth business. Your team members aren't inherently motivated by the experience of the fighting a good fight and that winning feeling that comes with growing. As a leader, you no longer have that inherent positive yet unspoken aura around your business. No doubt you have many techniques for reinvigorating your team. We're sure at different times during this plateau phase you have had positive response to your motivational speeches—yet the results have not been lasting.

So, it's time for something different, and radical. No more *I have a dream* speech. No more, *we choose to go to the moon* speech and the associated goals. The trick is *not* to ignore the goals but to focus on the things that need to be done to *move the needle* toward those goals—on a day-to-day basis. When we say move the needle, imagine the needle of a measuring instrument such as a speedometer.

We realize that a focus on the present—even though we are *not* encouraging you to be short-termist—may feel a little counter intuitive to you. Let's see what football coach Nick Saban has to say on this topic.

With six National Championships to his credit, University of Alabama football coach Nick Saban is one of the greatest college coaches of all time. Although his long-term goals are very clear to him, he says that the focus of the messaging to the team should not be about the outcome, the messaging is about what needs to be done to achieve the outcome. His current advice to his players is:

Don't think about winning the SEC Championship. Don't think about the national championship. Think about what you need to do in this drill, on this play, in this moment. That's the process: Let's think about how we can be the best in what we can do today, the task at hand.

In 2006 Nick also said: "We're not going to talk about *what* we're going to accomplish. We're going to talk about *how* we're going to do it."

So, how can that translate to your business? For each business, that will be different. Your business is unique. So we'll let you pause here for a moment to reflect on that.

Maybe an example will help you. If you run a hotel, your own goals are probably ambitious and forward looking. That's great. Yet, you know the future is highly dependent on how each employee delivers quality of service. And you have no doubt ensured that your employees already know of the importance of the quality of experience their guests experience. That's 101 in the hospitality business.

But if we apply what Nick Saban said above: "*That's the process: Let's think about how we can be the best in what we can do today, the task at hand.*" *So, for your hotel: To* what extent is the service the *best* it can be? Is that service delivered authentically or superficially? Is there pride in each interaction with the guest?

Written here in letters and words, the distinction between good customer service and the best customer service seems insignificantly small. *Yet, you know all too well the difference between lip service and good service is worlds apart, as is the impact. Only the latter causes your customer to say great things about you to others.* The success of online shoe retailer Zappos has been well documented: It went from a struggling start-up in 2000 to getting acquired by Amazon in a deal valued at $1.2 billion in 2009. Zappos started off as just an online shoe store in the United States, but always had a bigger desire: *to be a leader in customer experience.*

Zappos' founder and CEO Tony Hsieh didn't just say they will be a customer service leader, they made that the primary criteria for decision making, even in the types of people who want to work at Zappos. Customer Service is the company's central philosophy aimed at each employee on a day to day basis. So much so, Amazon bought them in the hope some of the philosophy would rub off...

Zappos' desire influences day-to-day behavior of each employee. It is a journey, not a destination for each employee. *And* it's not a superficial statement, as the organization truly embodies this desire. The CEO discussed this desire from the heart, on a regular basis. The organization put a lot of resources in place to ensure their systems and processes were aligned to this desire so that they *can be the best in what [they] can do today, the task at hand.*

Pause: Did you make notes of things in the Action This Today section in the back of this book? If not, please take this opportunity to review the prior pages to identify again any thoughts and ideas you want to follow up on.

CHAPTER 23

To Grow *Try This*...Which Right Things?

If you're feeling there are more behaviors that move the needle, you're right. Your experience rightly tells you that identifying the behaviors that help your team to do the right things isn't easy. How can we leaders be sure we've identified the right thing—that moves the needle? Which right things should our employees try to live each and every day?

Try This...Overcoming Invisible Opposing Forces

We like to work backwards from the desired goals. What are you trying to achieve?

And then let's look for behaviors that your employees perform that could really move the needle toward that goal. Understanding the importance and difficulty of that relationship must *not* be underestimated. But a good business leader like yourself shouldn't have any difficulty in putting your finger on that relationship, after a little—or perhaps a lot—of thoughtful contemplation.

Ah, don't forget that at the start of the Change section, we identified the Invisible Opposing Forces. Now we will deal with them. You'll likely achieve the best results if you look beyond the obvious relationships and look for the Invisible Opposing Forces! Let us refer you to another sport that some people call football, but you probably call soccer, then see what we can learn from Free Climbers and Southwest Airlines.

If you've ever watched soccer matches of the FIFA World Cup and seen tied games decided by soccer superstars taking and yet often missing penalty kicks, you might appreciate what we mean. Sure, they practice very hard indeed. During the training sessions they focus on, what Nick Saban would call, the task at hand. They have probably been playing soccer since they were knee-high to a grasshopper and have no doubt practiced taking these penalty kicks several thousands of times in their careers, some in very high pressure situations. The goal posts don't move, the spot for the penalty kick is in exactly the same place every time. So, why do they miss the spot kick in the final match itself when so much rides on that single kick?

Maybe Alex can help here. Alex Honnold is one of the *best* and most inspiring free climbers of the current climbing generation. Free climbers climb without any ropes or other equipment and by themselves. Since 2009, Alex had been thinking about free climbing El Capitan, almost 3,000 feet of vertical (or worse) rockface in Yosemite Valley.

For Alex, it became a goal notwithstanding the fact that five people have died on such climbing attempts in the last four years. Having a future-orientated goal doesn't mean you'll achieve it.

Of course Alex did all the right things with the task at hand. To achieve his goal, Alex identified the behavior he needed to exhibit on a daily basis. He spent four plus months specifically doing practice climbs of the most difficult stages of the route—for a climb that on the day took him less than four hours to complete. He planned his route meticulously, prepared for surprises, and also practiced climbs (with ropes) along the entire route for months. He had been climbing most of his life so there's plenty of practice and experience under his belt. Others that tried and failed to free climb El Capitan had also done the same or similar things in training, yet failed. Alex Honnold achieved his remarkable feat in June 2017 and attracted world media attention in a difficult sport. What was the difference?

Alex not only focused on the visible tasks at hand, but also identified the Invisible Opposing Force of fear. He succeeded at such a challenging task, due to his extraordinary ability to stay calm. In this situation, a lack of calmness could have dire consequences!

Beyond identifying the behaviors of each and every employee that enable the desired effect toward the desired goal, we're interested in those behaviors that not only move the needle the most but also tackle the Invisible Opposing Forces. It is remarkable to think about any company, especially an airline, running profitably for 43 years—not quarters— and counting. Southwest Airlines has been successful by connecting the employees' well-being—with a central theme of fairness on a day-to-day basis—to that of the airline's success.

> As the Freiburgs' write in their book (*Nuts! Southwest Airlines' Crazy Recipe for Business and Personal Success*): *The real secret to Southwest's success is having one of the most highly motivated and productive work-forces in the world. They are motivated by a sense of fairness that says—we want your well-being to be tied to the company's well-being because, after all, you are the company.*

In the last chapter we highlighted how Zappos did so well because the whole organization's systems were orientated towards allowing their employees to walk the walk of excellent customer service. Such an approach enables the needle to move towards growth. In this chapter we've highlighted the fact that sometimes those employee behaviors come from deeply rooted feelings of themselves, particularly if they need to overcome invisible opposing forces. We gave you some examples of calmness (as in taking soccer penalty kicks and free climbing) or feelings of a sense of fairness. Unfortunately, you and not this book, need to discover the magic sauce for your employees.

So what makes your employees tick and want to take the business to the next level? We think you're probably getting our gist now, knowing that growing your plateau business requires deeper thought and actions than first impressions.

Pause: Did you make notes of things in the Action This Today section in the back of this book? If not, please take this opportunity to review the prior pages to identify again any thoughts and ideas you want to follow up on.

CHAPTER 24

To Grow *Try This*...The Right Things, Self-Measured

OK, so you've delegated, introduced accountability, avoided chaos by focusing your team's energy on achieving the task at hand that moves the needle whilst overcoming the Invisible Opposing Forces, now what? Well, you already know that you achieve what you measure. So, let's measure whether your team is walking the walk, day to day.

No, we don't want any overcomplicated measurement tool. We just need a single daily threshold that each person can hold *themselves* accountable to. What is the single thing that your employees can use to self-measure themselves? It should be:

- Binary (with simple yes/no)
- Intuitive—each employee can be self-aware
- Helps employees to decide their behaviors in accordance with the metric

Walmart is ranked #1 in Forbes Global 500 list with revenues of around half a trillion dollars. Their strategic ambitions were always great, and Walmart's growth has become the stuff of legends. Working backwards from their desired strategic goal, the two things that stand out as being important to move the needle forward are:

- Scale: being large enough to command huge discounts from their suppliers, and being large enough to replicate their success in multiple geographies
- Focusing on everyday low prices

Scale creates a positive upward spiral that is enabled by the insistence on everyday low prices. Scale is not something the mass of employees can change. However a focus on everyday low prices is measurable by the employees themselves - we all know when we are being wasteful - and helps employees determine their own behaviors.

Walmart's founder Sam Walton was clear in his intentions about the kind of company that Walmart was going to be on a day-to-day basis. From the day he opened his first five-and-dime store in 1950, the business has focused on behaving in line with keeping prices as low as possible. He walked the walk of low everyday prices. So much so that "everyday low prices" is also Walmart's branding slogan clearly communicating their intentions to their customers even all these decades later.

> Walmart is known for being the provider of everyday low prices. Every action that every employee undertakes is grounded in that desire. For example, we're told Walmart office based employees empty their own trash bins at their desk at the end of each day. They don't spend money entertaining their employees or business partners. The employees even share bedrooms when they stay at hotels, to save money.

You will notice from the above examples of Zappos, Southwest, and Walmart, each and every employee can know and understand their role in their organization. Each employee can behave on a daily basis in a way that is consistent with their organization's desire. Each employee can walk the walk toward success. The employees don't need to wait to the end of the quarter to evaluate whether *they* are contributing toward providing best customer experience, contributing toward the organization's well-being, or providing everyday low prices. They can judge themselves, daily.

Try This...Feedback Loop

OK, if you find that the employees and you are striking yes—I did it daily—yet the businesses performance is not beginning to head toward the desired outcome...you may have to check which of these you need to go back to and tweak:

- Did we correctly understand the cause and effect relationship between our behaviors today and the future outcome we desire?

- Did we identify the behavior changes that move the needle (toward the desired outcome) and then make those changes?
- Did our behavioral change overcome/address the Invisible Opposing Force(s)?
- Did we delegate enough to the team to allow them to self-correct their own behaviors and address the Invisible Opposing Forces?
- Did we identify the right measurement, that is, usable on a day-to-day basis, and are we all using the scoring in the best way?

The above five questions are a good way to self-diagnose what might need further tweaking and revise your team's day-to-day behaviors, to get to the desired outcomes.

*Try This...*Revisiting the Vacation

Last time we mentioned vacations, it was to point out you aren't taking any...now we can think of vacations as a reward. Once your team is clear on the desired change and how they can walk the walk...consider letting your team (or the most senior subset of the team) manage their own vacation time. Set a new expectation such that they no longer need to ask you before planning their own vacation time, but they tell you as an FYI (For Your Information) once they have satisfied themselves that their absence won't disrupt how they interact and operate within the organization. This shows them you trust them to make the right choices, in line with the desired change and the positive results of accountability.

And eventually, consider stopping, even counting, the vacation days, obviously suggesting the employees themselves can manage things without disrupting the way of being of the organization. Let us know what happens.

Pause: Did you make notes of things in the Action This Today section in the back of this book? If not, please take this opportunity to review the prior pages to identify again any thoughts and ideas you want to follow up on.

CHAPTER 25

To Grow *Try This...*
Through Buy-In, Buy-In,
Buy-In

Unless you have acquired God-like properties, you can't be omnipresent, that is, in all places at once. It is also almost certainly true that you can in fact do all the tasks that together make up your business better than any of the individuals you've hired to do them. However, if your present activities can earn you $100 per hour, then comparative advantage says don't swap for a $20 per hour job, unless you are at least five times faster than the existing $20 jobholder.

That's simple economics.

And as we think we have demonstrated in this book, unless you delegate tasks and, through operational controls, accountability *and* trust, you are not going to expand beyond where you are now, other than marginally. If, however, there is team buy-in to a company wide aspiration, you have in effect got an army of mini-me's. Perhaps none quite as good as you, but nonetheless functioning for the good of the business without them needing to refer every single simple decision back to you.

How did you learn to ride a bike? Someone stood beside you to balance you, then ran alongside with one hand on the bike, providing stability, as you pedaled. Then suddenly, and probably without your knowledge, they let go and you pedaled on—on two wheels—yourself. And you probably went no further than the Wright Brothers did with early flights at Kitty Hawk—though you along the road, not through the air. Your cycle tutor trusted and you delivered, not immediately as elegantly as an Olympic cycling champion, but you moved your own cycling along.

Likewise, the results of trusting your team to make decisions for the business might initially not be as graceful as you would want it for yourself, but unless you involve others it is difficult to see how your business now as a Wright Flier 1 might ultimately morph into a Boeing jet.

If your team does walk the walk for the desired change for the business, then overwhelmingly the business will move forward. Of course things can and do go wrong. But they did when it was just you in the business as much as it does for corporations employing 100,000 plus people today. However, with the right team ethic, aspiration, trust—they are all interchangeable words—the overhead of a setback can be minimized.

When all said and done, it is possibly the fear of things going wrong that makes up a large portion of the reluctance to let go. However, a trusted team ought to be able to tell you the bad stuff as well as simultaneously fixing it. The alternatives of either not reporting failure or passing the issue to you for your exclusive fix are *not* places where you want your business to be.

Try This…a New Role for You?

We know a bioscientist who worked as CEO for a listed company giving it pretty much 24/7 attention at the expense of family and health. However, on borrowed time, he did lead his company to great things—sufficient for it to become the victim of a takeover. Our man's inevitable reward was redundancy and a move to his own start-up.

In the new company, he took a lot of time out from normal CEO activity to make his direct reports the best they could be in their own disciplines as well as empowering them with much of the decision-making authority the CEO would normally reserve for himself. He now works full time in his start-up, that's two and a half days a week, encouraging the team via aspiration and thereafter being available for PR and investor relations—both often receiving scant service by other, far busier, CEOs.

Somewhere in there is a very important message. A new you could seriously improve your productivity in total and be able to focus on areas not previously receiving sufficient of your attention. We bet if you own a restaurant, a weekly piece for your local news outlets *from the kitchen* would bring more trade to your door. If you are any sort of professional, a *daily thought of the day* posted onto your community's website will encourage the readers to think first of you when needing your type of service.

Even for our widget man, you will know that you exhibit at the same exhibitions each year as you want to be seen, ignoring the fact that every other widget company is also showing its wares. A new you might be the answer. Perhaps, put your exhibition stand up in the back of a truck and use some of your two and a half days of work driving it to important prospects' premises. Then perhaps it is not five-minutes attention from one visitor at the show, it might be all day for half the prospect's staff. Wow. Half the company now lobbying for your widgets? Umm, we smell the money.

Pause: Did you make notes of things in the Action This Today section in the back of this book? If not, please take this opportunity to review the prior pages to identify again any thoughts and ideas you want to follow up on.

CHAPTER 26

To Grow *Try This*...With an Acquisition

Built on an effective aspiration it might be that you want to contemplate growing the business further by an acquisition. An acquisition, whether for a disrupter entrepreneur or for slower organic growth company, is potentially the sort of Trojan horse, step-change that might work very well for you. Conversely if you are selling your business and an acquisition is not something you are minded to consider, you might find some useful thoughts below—though probably as reversed thoughts. In fact even if you are maintaining the status quo, there are still nuggets to be discovered as we review things that increase or destroy value.

Don't rush off at this moment to go and buy your nearest rival (or sell to your nearest competitor). They'll probably have seen you coming and are ready to extract a fancy price. Neither should you (necessarily) go and acquire the business that you know appears to be bargain priced. In this latter case there has to be a reason for the price: If it really was that good a deal, why didn't someone else in your industry, trade, or profession snap it up long before it came to your attention?

Cynics of business, cynics in your own line of business, and simply people that have done them will tell you that acquisitions rarely deliver fully on expectations. There are lots of reasons for this. But top of the list, and here's why you don't do it yet, is that the buyer is invariably wearing the famous rose-tinted spectacles at the time of the acquisition.

And here it's you who is the buyer.

So to make sure you are wearing the right spectacles—it's sunglasses by the way, and we'll come back to those later—we are going to look at the whole DNA around an acquisition before we don the glasses.

We're not convinced we've tempered your enthusiasm enough so far. So please remember that an acquisition is really just another make or buy decision where you are about to choose *buy*. With this being so, please, please remember that you also have the *ignore* option. And whatever you do, don't get yourself suckered into an acquisition because you have to. As an example, one of the authors worked for a telephone handset whole-saler. The CEO saw the opportunity to acquire an underperforming rival. To the CEO's credit, he involved many of his current team in investigating the proposed business or *undertaking due diligence* for those more legally minded. However, the sales director and credit controller took the view that if the acquisition was occurring, there was no reason why our company couldn't sell products to this rival—who had otherwise been on credit stop. By the time this was picked up, our rival owed us a huge sum of money and they in turn made it clear that unless the acquisition occurred, they'd be forced into liquidation and our company would be that sum out of pocket.

We did reduce the purchase price to reflect this, but in reality we should have walked away. The message we learned was to tread carefully—so carefully our next piece of corporate activity was to sell another part of the business.

So why would you want to make an acquisition?

Synergy

Synergy is by far the number one reason for making an acquisition. Two plus two equals five. Yes, it's true. Two businesses combined only need one CEO, one set of premises perhaps, one sales force, one widget making machine, but will have two lots of customers—so a doubling of customers combined with one set of shared costs really can perform a magical trans-formation to one's bottom line.

However, and didn't you just know we were going to say that, *if you are the acquirer, you really, really have to make sure that the costs are set on the trajectory to oneness.* Before you commit to acquiring, how exactly are you going to get out of the lease on the acquired premises you're not going to want? What is the people plan in the face of your expanded manage-ment—*expanded* because you'll want some of *their* best people in your top team, won't you? And having got the best ones, what are their plans to cut the combined number of posts and so achieve the goal? We'll labor this point. Managers don't like surprises and know from real-world experience it is often easier to keep people JIC rather than fight later for the right to hire additional heads. JIC also covers over the fact that managers will have skimped their due diligence duties and probably don't know in sufficient detail what many of the acquired staff's day-to-day work is about. Or even that the hire in question is part of moving the business forward at all.

One of the authors holds his hands up on this one. During a software company acquisition, he fought really hard and ultimately successfully to retain an acquired employee on the grounds he knew all the complexities around most of the historic ongoing business. Days after, it became clear that one could upgrade these historic customers to the current product line and that the knowledge holder's lock on the data was bypassed and that his special knowledge was not necessary going forward.

Moving along the Value Chain

Everyone talks about *the supply chain.* These are the steps between the raw material and the end customer. Even if, as we have assumed, you manufacture widgets, it is surely not the case that, at one end, you dig the iron ore and coking coal out of the ground to make the necessary steel, nor, at the consumer end, you sell the thing-a-me-jig your widget is in, to Mrs. Mayweather in the Mall? Along the way, and at each step, processes occur—even as simple as barcode scanning at the till. Remember that margin on the overall sale is taken out by each step's processor. So it stands to reason there is margin upstream or downstream to your piece—either behind or in front of you in the supply chain—that can be acquired and its extra margin, at least in part, added to your bottom line.

Do be excited, they are sensible places to look. The cautionary tales are those of scale and relevance. You might use a lot of screws in the assembly of your widgets, but find that actually you are only taking one-thousandth of your screw manufacturer's production. So acquiring the screw manufacturer would be disproportional to your requirements *and* 99.9 percent of your newly acquired production would need to find customers not connected to your own widgets. Should some of these others be rival widget manufacturers, you might lose their business just as you begin to relish the opportunity to turn the price screw (sorry) on them.

If you don't find widgets to your liking, think about the consequences of buying an organic farm to support your organic restaurant. The chances are with your location, you'll have a limited growing and cropping season—facing surpluses for a few short weeks and the trouble of disposing of the excess, and many months of the year still buying in supplies from elsewhere.

Going the other way, to retail, always looks an attractive option because in almost every chain this is where the highest proportion of the end user price is syphoned off for what seems like the easiest task. Retail can be a success, but remember, though, high margins in retail come from dealing with pernickety consumers (not logical B2B customers) who often make unwarranted returns to expensive-to-run retail outlets and who expect to be able to select from a variety of brands—not just yours. Sure, the web reduces some of these costs, but then remember that, on the web, people have to find you, and then you will typically have to incentivize them to select from you alone. So we don't believe retailing is necessarily all it's cracked up to be from a profits source perspective, unless you like being a shopkeeper.

Geography

Doing something in business you shouldn't used to be said to be taking coals to Newcastle. Of the one hundred plus Newcastles around the planet, the Newcastle in question is in the United Kingdom. And of its two, it is Newcastle upon Tyne rather than Newcastle under Lyme. The expression is premised on the fact that behind Newcastle, in the county of Northumberland, there were once a huge number of efficient coal pits. Today, post Margaret Thatcher's 1980s government, post the decline of coal as a fuel, there are no mines operating within striking distance of this once remarkable coal-exporting port. So today, for the more limited users of coal, taking coals to Newcastle is actually necessary. Coal itself is both bulky and, as fuel goes, relatively cheap, so trucking a ton of the stuff for a Tynesider's household is not hugely economical for a business many miles away and therefore best distributed on a local basis.

At the other end of the value per transaction spectrum, realtors (United States)/estate agents (United Kingdom) also typically only work parochially, but for them location is not based on the cost of sending out property particulars but the more hands-on elements of their trade.

So there can be good reasons for having local depots, local representation, or whatever as part of an expansion plan. Acquiring a similar business to yours in different geography then makes sense. You will still only need one CEO and so on, but you will require duplicated equipment and people to deliver at the cutting edge. Plus, *and* be careful here, you might start breeding a new cost of someone(s) to be regional this or that, running up extensive mileages somehow coordinating these otherwise rudderless locations.

In math, we see this much more as two plus two equals four, but if the second two (and indeed third, fourth, etc., two) can be acquired economically, then you can still build a good bottom line.

Another win–win from geography can be that the cost of operations—mainly thinking here people and premises—might be significantly lower in another geography and you can move back office or production to this other location and become more competitive. A friend of the authors expanded his accounting practice by acquisition from simply being in the equivalent of San Francisco to then also active in Jackson, MS, where average wages are only about two-thirds of the former location but the bookkeeping staff are at least as good at their jobs. This obviously allows him to offer back office support to clients in the high price area at better prices.

Deal Structure

All acquisitions are different. However, it is a good bet that the business you acquire is sold to you by its owner who is probably also the most senior person (in status) in the acquired business and is selling because of whatever reason they prefer your offer of stuff (be it upfront cash or stock, shares, or whatever), to them continuing to run the business to extract cash as salary or dividends over time. After a handover, their likely preferred option is to disappear out of the business completely, which is immediately a positive step toward any synergy you desire.

We've said *stuff* above—because as illustrated it doesn't have to be cash. We'll deal with this stuff properly, later. However, sometimes it is cash that does all the talking. This is almost always the case when you are looking to acquire a business from an administrator/liquidator. These folks are appointed to extract cash for the benefit of creditors and often within that category, for specific secured creditors. Money to pay their own fees also has to be generated, so that to maximize the underlying cash recovered versus costs ratio, they are looking for quick, cash, deals.

In these instances, you are only buying those assets you want, typically some of the brand, stock, equipment, and customers, and from a holistic approach, abandoning staff not required and obligations of all sorts—for premises, to the tax authorities, to the other company's bank or other creditors. The liquidator/administrator will push you for a quick decision and they'll push you on price. We wouldn't want to accuse them of providing misleading guidance, but please write and tell us if you ever find them telling you that you are the only bidder. Let them see early on that you do have access to the money and that you are prepared to deal. In return, use every waking moment on due diligence—if in doubt start with customers; at least then, heaven forbid, if you don't proceed with the purchase, you might instead have an insight into some prospectively rosy future sales for yourself!

We once had the opportunity to pick over the corpse of an auto dealer. Their parts inventory contained a lot of readily saleable items for a franchise we held of the same marque nearby, so we encouraged our acquiring team to concentrate on valuing the collapsed business' 100 best-selling lines. The 100 incidentally being our best sellers, not necessarily that of the corpse business. Our offer for those—based on 25 percent of what we'd have to pay elsewhere—was sufficiently above other bids that the liquidator invited us to offer an extra 1 percent for the remainder of the stock and clear it all for him. That extra yielded tens of thousands of later value.

And that's all we took. Well nearly. We rather think the service manager at our place somehow found a customer list in the carnage and that list somehow got packed up with the parts. Later he somehow managed to use the list to make the demised dealer's former customers a new offer for the servicing of their autos.

In these situations, be picky, but better, be selective based on what your due diligence of their information throws up. You can't win it if you're not in it and you don't want the booby prize, however well it is dressed up.

Sunglasses

We're majoring on acquisitions, because sooner or later you're going to get suckered into one (or more). Sure they can be good for your business and the underlying math works, provided always they deliver on promises. If they do, you're home free, scot free, or simply out of jail. Our concerns therefore naturally focus around the negatives, to alert you best we can, to the existence of bumps in the road, circling vultures, amassing sharks, and the odd snake in the grass.

So please forgive the emphasis—the rose-tinted spectacles must be thrown away. Sunglasses are de rigueur. The other side mustn't see the whites of your eyes. There's a high-stakes game of poker to be played. And it will almost certainly only be about the price to be paid. But just as in real poker one can go *all in*, that is to say, stake everything, so one can also fold. When negotiating an acquisition, one can similarly opt not to play the hand, or *ignore* in our earlier parlance—provided of course there is no legal commitment to go ahead.

> If ever the lawyers' immortal words "subject to contract," were important, it is in the negotiation of an acquisition. Used up front on any exchange of correspondence, throughout the due diligence stage, right up to the moment you sign on the dotted line. And please, even when the dotted line is placed in front of you, please, please don't sign unless you are 100 percent sure that you have got both the best deal you can and that the deal really, really works for you. Don't ever let inertia, peer pressure, or the amount of money and time you've expended up to contracts stage be any part of any reason you choose to sign.

Reasons Not to Sign

Stage one: Articulate clearly and succinctly what the business you are going to acquire does and who it does it to. Add on to this summation a statement of what you want to achieve from it post acquisition and create some success criteria by which you will measure how both businesses (yours and the target) come through the process. Can't do it? Then don't proceed. Can do it? Write it down—you might look back on it later—and laugh or cry.

Stage two: Break the target into bite-sized chunks. That's probably best done by functional area, for example, sales, marketing, production, and distribution. In turn, this should be based on how the target is organized rather than your existing business, so that nothing is lost in translation and all the pieces you're examining collectively add to the totality. Then look at the pieces. Do you like *everything* you see? If not, don't do it.

Stage three. Get stuck in to understanding (where *understanding* is the summation of both learning and application) both the helicopter height view *and* the nitty, gritty, deep-down dirty detail of each of your chunks above. By all means, get yourself an acquisition checklist. No do, but don't look at it simply as a shopping list, because in addition—and let us reinforce the word—you need understanding.

Are you understanding how this possible acquisition really, really works? And if so can you kindly tell us, now and honestly, why the vendor wants to sell? And if that reason doesn't chime with you, don't do it.

Why go to all this bother?

What's it all about, really? Let's kick some tires.

Sales Analysis

More than any other single thing, you will want to know where the sales come from. Here, 80/20 will almost certainly apply so for the 20 percent of customers who make up 80 percent of the target's business, please give 80 percent of your attention. Sure, per the checklist, you will want to know how they order, when they order, what prices they pay, when they pay, who they are, how to contact them, and so on, but that's all mechanical. Does the current boss have a special relationship? Do they enjoy some special treatment—not recorded in the company's records? We're thinking here of customers being taken to trade shows, given exclusives, supplied uninvoiced additional product, offered marketing support, loaned some of our target's staff, and so on. Will they remain with the business under new management? Illustratively, we always find ourselves pondering if ladies-who-lunch would still go to Alfonso's hair salon if Alfonso sold out to Jacqui? OK, you are not buying a hairdresser, but will some of the bigger customers leave under your new management?

And always suspect. Years ago, a pal of ours had a fire. It destroyed a large proportion of his business premises. To help recover, his major supplier extended his payment terms by several months. About a year later, with our pal still paying about two months behind the norm (the business was recovering slowly), his major supplier bribed him (with clever discounting) to bring himself as up-to-date as everyone else, just so they could tell the buyer of *their* business that no one was, or had been, behind with payments. It wasn't strictly true, but it seemed to be what it said in the books. Needless to say, under the new management, our pal again had to extend payment terms as he'd basically robbed Peter to pay Paul, to achieve the required catch-up.

Everything we previously said about your customers in this book is also relevant. Which ones cause problems, which ones only pay for the last order when they want the next one, and so on? You need to know this. You might even use this information as part of your poker game, to get a better price.

Stock, Not Inventory

Nothing is more open to abuse than inventory. Or do we mean stock? Why such different words for the same thing? There is no difference—they're interchangeable. Your vendor will doubtless show you some sort of stock-take record as part of due diligence—that will give you a value at the bottom, of that stock when it was counted. Doubtless there will need to be another count a lot closer to your take-over time. That will tick some boxes on the acquisition checklist, but it won't stop you being fleeced. Consider some of these howlers:

- The hollow tower or pallet: For most stock in bulk it is easy to stack (or store on a pallet), where all sides are solid but the center's hollow. So a quoted "5 by 5 equals 25 to a layer" could easily be just the 16 around the outside.
- The forklift scam: After you have counted, or checked on an item, a forklift comes along and transports the stock in

question to another part of the store so you can count it (or
check it) again. May be by turning a pallet around, it can look
different from the reverse?

- Double-counting: It is easy, accidentally or deliberately, for
two sets of counters to both count the same thing and so it
gets put on the list twice. Maybe in a warehouse, counting the
same thing from different sides.
- Wrong measuring: At a superstore count, the butchery department put the weight of a beef carcass in pounds in the quantity column, but the value of the whole side of beef in the price
column. Later, this item found itself overvalued 578 times!

And that's just about doing the stock-take, to tick the box on the
checklist. How about getting to understand the detail? First, go physically
look, so that the top 20 (we suggest in most places—but this time it is
20 as a number, not a percentage) of stock items by value are known to
you and that therefore you can tell if the stock evaluation is of the right
magnitude for these items. Next, just because it is *in stock* doesn't mean
it has any value to the business. It might have been acquired from the
Mayflower in the seventh century and lain idle ever since. So alongside
any evaluation, you want to know the stock-turn for an item. Depending
on your trade, anything representing more than say three months' worth
should be reduced in value or not counted at all.

Finally here, what about customer returns? They might have been
repaired, repacked, or whatever, but if they form part of the stock valu-
ation, first is there a non-rose-tinted explanation of how they are going
to be turned back into money and second, does that methodology work
on its own or will it cannibalize new sales or undermine the value of the
new product in your customers' eyes? If in doubt, seek a reduction in
inventory value and ultimately a reduction in the price you are prepared
for the business.

Creditors and Liabilities

If you are acquiring another company (as opposed to buying assets from
a liquidator), you are buying it warts and all. As part of the acquisition

there will be a sale and purchase agreement and in that your vendor will warrant to you that they have disclosed all the liabilities and further that they'll make restitution if not true and brought to their subsequent attention, assuming, of course, you use a commercial lawyer and these things are agreed. That *doesn't mean* you ignore liabilities; on the contrary, they deserve the same attention, but, defensively, as customers.

Here are a few thoughts arising from some of our battle scars:

- The vendor disappears. A cunning plan where the vendor says everything is peachy (we've overused *rosy*), extracts a fine price from you, then disappears. You find problems and he's not around to pay you back. If you have any doubts on peachiness or later invisibility, talk to your lawyer about a retention, holding some of the price back where, under the problem circumstances, you would expect to be able to reclaim it.

- Never forget the property. Many acquisition success plans hinge on getting rid of the acquired company's property. So you will need to know it has proper ownership, has planning permission, and is woodworm free or whatever free and you will have to be lucky enough to find a new taker for the premises. If it's on a lease, remember too that the landlord is going to need to approve the new tenant who may have to agree new terms with the landlord, perhaps making it hard to re-let. Consider using a property surveyor to do your property due diligence for you, but again use your eyes too—if you think something's not right, it probably isn't.

- Other contracts. *Change of ownership* clauses are becoming more common in contracts generally. Is it in any of your target's customer contracts? Is it in any of the supplier contracts or any important service contracts? Will the vendor let you seek the reassurances you need, direct and prior to completing the purchase, yourself and in writing that post the transaction, things will continue as before?

- Debtors in creditors. It is not uncommon for there to be some debtors, that is, some negative balances, in the supplier's ledger. Their effect is to lower the total value of the list, so you the acquirer think there are fewer liabilities. An example of this was a construction company acquisition. The stated creditors were $80,000 but that had only been calculated after including a minus $25,000 from an overpaid, and now bankrupt, concrete supplier. So it actually cost $105,000 to pay the bills. It is important therefore for each negative balance you first need to know if the supplier sees it the same way—if not, the chances are your target is either not keeping good records or that they're simply missing an invoice or two and thereby overstating profitability. If this is the case, then no money will ever be refunded from the supplier and so the real amounts owing are higher. Second, if it really is money owed back to the business, you need to assess the creditworthiness of the supplier and thus again whether you'll ever see it as cash— or be able to spend it with that supplier on future things for the business—which we couldn't do with the concrete supplier.

- Potential legal issues outstanding. Has a customer claimed to have been food-poisoned? Is an ex-employee suing for an accident at work or discrimination...

Rights to Do

We've mentioned earlier change of ownership in terms of customers but in fact there is a far larger list of *rights* held by third parties you need to consider. The business you acquire may well be a franchise: Think burger joint, gas station, Century 21...the list is long. To protect the franchise, the franchisor, and not the guy trying to sell to you, will need to ensure that you will uphold the franchise reputation. This might involve vetting, formal approval, and, in almost every circumstance, a fee. Even if not a franchise, the business name or a brand name might be licensed from a previous owner and that license agreement needs to be assessed.

Thinking back to the widgets, are they the business' own development or are the rights to make them owned by someone else? Make sure you ask the vendor "What licenses and approvals will I need to carry on your business?" and then at every stage of every piece of due diligence, keep your enquiring eyes wide open. The vendor might not be aware of some of them himself—we can't expect him to remember everything. We the authors were seeking to inexpensively acquire a school teaching aids business, only to discover that the expensive monthly rental contract on the photocopier had seven years to run, before we could cancel it!

Please, please remember, your desire to know vastly outweighs the vendor's ability to remember. So probe for answers, not distractions. Worse that the only reason the vendor is letting go is that you are paying more than he thinks he would get from anyone else. So look under every rock, challenge every assumption, make every piece of bad news lower the purchase price...and still be prepared to walk away.

Post-Acquisition Plan and Review

We've touched on this already. If you are really determined to make an acquisition, then find time *before* signature to create yourself a post-acquisition checklist. This will be your document with timelines indicating what needs to happen post-acquisition, by whom and when, to bring your about-to-be acquired business into your stable. Look at the dependencies—if for instance you want to be out of some premises in six months, when should you appoint someone to start marketing it, contacting the landlord for approval, hiring a removal team, and so on. Ask yourself what comes to form the critical path and—at the risk of overworking the word—who is critical to the process and what safeguards do you have in place to assure you they're not about to leave or take an extended break for whatever reason.

The checklist needs to be finished off with some performance criteria—which should be measurable—to be your target for the new (or the combined) business. It could be headcount, percentage overhead, cash in the bank, sales—or indeed measures for all of them, and the all-important date when each of these things will be measured.

When you have made the acquisition, look at your document. Strongly resist the urge to bin it when you conclude it is not relevant. Because we bet you, you'll be looking for more entries from the bumper book of excuses again to rationalize why you have abandoned the plan.

However irrelevant, conduct the review as at the date you originally envisaged. Look at the nonsensical data produced. Really look. There are in amongst the promises made before, and the delivery and execution after, some really valid things to learn for when you do it again. And don't say never again. Remember life's a bitch and Sod's law will ensure you really do end up doing it all over again in the future.

We're human. We never learn.

Paying with "Stuff"

There is no doubt that *Cash is King*. If you buy something, and you've paid for it, then it's yours to do as you wish with. That's great apart from the fact that, in our experience, cash is invariably in very short supply. So what are the options?

There are basically two alternatives to paying in full, immediately with cash. The first option is to defer the payment and the second option is to spread the payment over the rest of all time.

At first glance, option one looks to be favorite. In many acquisitions, the buyer will not see the same value as the vendor in the anticipated future income stream. This is usually dealt with by the vendor and purchaser agreeing to there being some deferred or contingent consideration to be based both on a delay in time and upon the performance of the business being acquired under the new management. As we have also identified elsewhere it may be the case that some of the consideration is simply deferred to be held as a warranty reserve so that if any of the vendor's representations turn out to be incorrect, the buyer has access to funds for redress.

Now it is true that a strong vendor will seek to have as much of the above deferred cash as possible in a safe pair of hands which usually equates to an escrow agreement with one of the lawyers in the transaction. However, a strong buyer will be able to convince the other side—that the buyer himself holds the cash. And for the purposes of this book we are talking to you as the buyer. So let's assume that you convinced the seller that some of the money they expect to take away on sale date will come to them later. So why not in fact press the case that all the cash in this transaction should be later and suggest instead that the vendor take loan notes from you the buyer. In this case, the loan notes will probably be for a fixed term and you will have to give them an interest rate coupon. However, if you plan it properly, not only can the acquired business cover the interest payments but it would also allow you to amass enough cash to redeem the loan notes when they mature. Effectively acquiring the business for nothing!

The other choice we introduced earlier was to pay for the business for ever. Here, we are thinking that you the buyer could issue the vendor equity, that is, stock/shares in your business. If the seller is convinced that you are going to do great things with his business and your business combined, then by giving him a slice of the action he might be persuaded to take no cash at all. For him, on the plus side, he gets growth in the value of the stock/shares based on your performance and, if you're minded to pay them, by the receipt of dividends. His downside of course is that you might not make any money at all in the future and his shares become worthless. For you, there is the emotional challenge of giving away part of your business to someone who is probably not going to contribute anything further into the future. For some, this is a complete no-no but for others it is recognition of the contribution of a valuable building block at the time when that block was helpful to your growth.

Of course all three elements—cash, loan notes, and equity—can be mixed and matched to suit the circumstances. It was only in the now defunct U.K. Woolworths' loose confectionery department there was a sign that said: Quality Street is *not* pick'n'mix.

Pause: Did you make notes of things in the Action This Today section in the back of this book? If not, please take this opportunity to review the prior pages to identify again any thoughts and ideas you want to follow up on.

Summary

For Britain in 1940, the Second World War must have seemed very dark indeed. It had to bring its defeated troops back from Dunkirk, and the German Luftwaffe was reducing London to rubble through the Blitz. Britain must have, to almost every man, woman, and child, feared mightily for the country's and their own futures not knowing if the United States would ever come to the party (which of course it did a year later, after Pearl Harbor).

That *almost* excluded one key man, that of Winston Churchill. On a diet which seemed to be a fat cigar, a bottle of Scotch whisky, and no more than two hours sleep a day, he maintained that the Allies would prevail. He had to totally rely on delegation to have army, navy, and air force perform. That delegatees would turn UK manufacturing into a well-oiled supply chain and that others would raise food production over and over to help feed the nation. He needed others to develop and work convoys that brought necessary imports in, which kept the people alive and the war machine in business.

Perhaps his greatest own contribution was to ensure bright ideas happened. He knew that dithering or procrastination would cost time and lives, so for things that needed his affirmative decision he would pen Action This Day on his instruction memos. It was his first world war role that saw the invention of the tank, his support for science that saw DNA analyzed, as prime minister he approved the famous bouncing bomb, and so on. Through the possible expedient of diarizing a copy of the action memo, he had a control to ensure he could confirm these things occurred.

So why should you dither? We know there isn't the expediency of a war, but are you surely returning to our bumper book of excuses if you are not already doing some things differently? We're sure you would have nodded along to a lot of suggestions in this book, but have you taken any one of them anywhere, beyond saying to yourself: That's a good idea.

Let's remember that you are here because you feel your business has reached, and is not moving, above a plateau—that somehow a glass ceiling exists keeping you where you are today. But we are all agreed you want to do something about it—so really, why don't you add some thoughts to Action This Today, now?

OK, so maybe it is our fault. We have within our text caused you to stop and hold your breath more than once. We suggested you might stop and see if the impediment to growth is actually you or maybe people acquired for one purpose but now just hanging on because of *your* inertia. We queried whether you had people on board where outsourcing might be better and whether people you have, have ideas you should listen to.

We suggested the product or service might be holding you back. We asked impertinently if it could be simplified, replaced with software, or even abandoned altogether. If not that, we wondered if you were focused on the wrong customers, the problem makers, and the ones who simply take advantage. If you also said *no* to all of those, we considered all the monetary aspects, from holding too much of the wrong inventory to getting the price wrong and ignoring possible financial assistance out there.

We even contemplated whether you really wanted to be in *your* business at all.

Having eliminated the wrongs—all the reasons we were asking you to stop—we contemplated change, more positively. We had a cornucopia of great suggestions. You might remember reference to the treasure map and its special locations: Organic Beach, Integration Peak, Geographic Cove, Doubling Bay, Sellup Landing, Hooksky Island, and Lottery Lagoon.

It was about here too we raised the thorny issue of your idle website and miniscule contribution to social media. You could argue it didn't fit in at this juncture, but that beautifully reflects the disruptive nature of the Internet *and* your head-in-the-sand reaction to it.

All of the foregoing was assuming you wanted to be in the widget business at all. So we challenged the basic tenet of whether you should actually make them or have that done by others. Heresy perhaps, but you were not pre-ordained to spend a life making them.

As if that wasn't enough, we got to mention some other useful growth vehicles—growth in capacity, growth with new hires, international expansion, and licensing. All great in their own right but none producing the step-change you wanted for your business. And suggested a fresh pair of eyes might help.

So it came to be that we mentioned the delegation, controls, and accountability, focusing on identifying which right things done daily, measured by your people, lead toward the desired strategic goals. Now, whilst you could criticize us, the authors, for not warning you of their arrival, think about it for a minute. If section one started with these topics, you would never have bought the book. Instead we suggested changing a punctured tire would allow you to improve the remainder of your journey. Surely, allegorically, that is the key to unlock your business and move it to the next level? The very thing we promised with the title.

Altering our course, we labored on growth via acquisition partly because it happens a lot and it rarely produces the desired outcome. We provided pages of be-awares that not only minimize the risks of an acquisition going awry, but which might actually reduce the price you pay, or in the wrong circumstance, allow you to walk away. And all this good stuff is doubly good. No, not an author's ego trip but the fact that, stood on its head, it is a great guide should you wish to sell rather than buy.

In amongst this whole book, the word *trust* emerges. Perhaps that will be your mantra going forward? You trust yourself with your business decisions and if you think about it, you trusted yourself with your choice of people you've hired into the business. So why not in turn trust those people to have the business's best interests at heart as they go about their work? Within an aspiration and with controls around your delegation of course.

It will work. Try it and be surprised.

About the Authors

Michael Carter qualified as a chartered accountant in the United Kingdom with KPMG, but became cynical of the audit process and leapt out into commerce at the first opportunity. He has created, developed, bought, and sold businesses and spent most of the last 20 years helping other people's start-ups and small companies. This is his fifth business book.

Karl Shaikh has a never-ending thirst for learning. He is curious, challenges perspectives, and enjoys identifying new hypotheses to test. At the heart of his curiosity is the question: How can we make any team, and thereby any organization, more successful? He has worked in many large corporations in strategic roles. Like Michael, he has started and grown businesses. He has worked with many entrepreneurs and assisted a number of non-profit organizations' boards. Learn more at www.1unknown.com

Michael and Karl came together in 2003 when they cofounded Virtual Directors Limited (VDL), a London-based consultancy. Initially business was slow. But when the pitch became "A consultancy that helps recruiters top line, bottom line and keeping key staff," VDL found itself retained by five different companies in as many weeks.

Both have travelled extensively, supporting businesses at different times on five continents. They have also become quite adept at selling businesses. They obtained a $1 million plus for a software company where the owner had anticipated liquidation and almost a $1 million more than the asking price for a lighting company where the outgoing owner used the proceeds to create a tennis academy in the south of France.

They hope some of their thoughts, approaches, and methodologies in this book will help you achieve what you aspire to.

Now It's Your Turn

Put this book down and see how much you can adopt of what you've read, in the next four hours. Be bold—it's there for the taking. Once you feel you've made all the progress you can, come back and read this book again. You'll notice that different questions pique your curiosity, partly because your mind will then be grappling with different Opposing Forces and also because you will have a deeper appreciation of some of the next issues to deal with. And then there is the random element, the inexplicably different things which now seem relevant. You'll find yourself creating a new Action This Today list, and that's a good thing. Over time, you will have become your own plateau buster.

Good luck!

Action This Today

Please describe below the ideas that you feel you can implement today, this week, or this month. Add multiple additional lines under the same heading if that area is your focus. But don't stop there, please adapt the table below to suit your own needs.

Stop—What If...It's Your People	☐ Action this today ☐ . . . . next week ☐ . . . . next month
Stop—What If...It's the Product	☐ Action this today ☐ . . . . next week ☐ . . . . next month
Stop—What If...It's the Customers	☐ Action this today ☐ . . . . next week ☐ . . . . next month
Stop—What If...It's the Money	☐ Action this today ☐ . . . . next week ☐ . . . . next month
Stop—What If...It's the Price	☐ Action this today ☐ . . . . next week ☐ . . . . next month
Stop—You Do Something Different	☐ Action this today ☐ . . . . next week ☐ . . . . next month
Change—The People Inside	☐ Action this today ☐ . . . . next week ☐ . . . . next month
Change—The Product	☐ Action this today ☐ . . . . next week ☐ . . . . next month
Change—The Customers	☐ Action this today ☐ . . . . next week ☐ . . . . next month
Change—The Price Model	☐ Action this today ☐ . . . . next week ☐ . . . . next month

Change—Money Matters	☐ Action this today ☐ .... next week ☐ ..... next month
Change—The Process	☐ Action this today ☐ .... next week ☐ ..... next month
Change—Other Stuff	☐ Action this today ☐ .... next week ☐ ..... next month
Grow—From Here	☐ Action this today ☐ .... next week ☐ ..... next month
Grow—Delegation And Controls	☐ Action this today ☐ .... next week ☐ ..... next month
Grow—Do The Right Things Now	☐ Action this today ☐ .... next week ☐ ..... next month
Grow—Which Right Things	☐ Action this today ☐ .... next week ☐ ..... next month
Grow—The Right Things Self-Measured	☐ Action this today ☐ .... next week ☐ ..... next month
Grow—Buy-In, Buy-In, Buy-In	☐ Action this today ☐ .... next week ☐ ..... next month
Grow—With An Acquisition	☐ Action this today ☐ .... next week ☐ ..... next month

Index

www.ingramcontent.com/pod-product-compliance
Lightning Source LLC
Chambersburg PA
CBHW061325220326
41599CB00026B/5039